EDITED BY KEVIN HICKSON

REBUILDING SOCIAL DEMOCRACY

Core principles for the centre left

T0339265

POLICY PRESS SHORTS INSIGHTS

First published in Great Britain in 2016 by

Policy Press
University of Bristol
1-9 Old Park Hill
Bristol
BS2 8BB
UK
t: +44 (0)117 954 5940
pp-info@bristol.ac.uk
www.policypress.co.uk

North America office:
Policy Press
c/o The University of Chicago Press
1427 East 60th Street
Chicago, IL 60637, USA
t: +1 773 702 7700
f: +1 773 702 9756
sales@press.uchicago.edu
www.press.uchicago.edu

British Library Cataloguing in Publication Data
A catalogue record for this book is available from the British Library.

Library of Congress Cataloging-in-Publication Data
A catalog record for this book has been requested.

ISBN 978-1-4473-3317-3 (paperback)
ISBN 978-1-4473-3320-3 (ePub)
ISBN 978-1-4473-3319-7 (Mobi)

Cover design by Policy Press
Front cover: image kindly supplied by www.alamy.co.uk
Printed and bound in Great Britain by CMP, Poole
Policy Press uses environmentally responsible print partners

Contents

Contributors

Judi Atkins is a lecturer in politics at Coventry University

Matt Beech is a senior lecturer in politics and Director of the Centre for British Politics at the University of Hull

Simon Griffiths is a senior lecturer in politics at Goldsmiths, University of London

Peter Hain is a Labour Peer, formerly MP for Neath (1991–2015) and a Cabinet Minister

Kevin Hickson is a senior lecturer in British politics at the University of Liverpool

Jasper Miles is completing his PhD at the University of Liverpool

Robert M. Page is Reader in democratic socialism and social policy at the University of Birmingham

Pete Redford is completing his PhD at the University of Birmingham

Emily Robinson is a senior lecturer in politics at the University of Sussex

Foreword: rediscovering confidence and soul

Peter Hain[1]

Why have social democratic parties been in abject retreat at the very time when inequality has been so remorselessly widening, real wages for the middle and working class declining and financial capitalism plagued by instability?

Of course frustration with social democratic parties is nothing new. The 1906 British general election sent 29 Labour MPs to the House of Commons. Yet, just two years after this pioneering political development, the leader of London's dockers Ben Tillett issued a pamphlet entitled *Is the Parliamentary Party a Failure?*[2]

A healthy impatience for progress has certainly been one of the Labour membership's key characteristics from the very start, guarding against complacency and what Ernest Bevin called 'poverty of ambition'. But it is acutely relevant to European social democracy today where centre-left parties seem to have lost faith in their own philosophy, leaving voters wondering what they stand for and whose side they are on.

In Britain former Labour Deputy Leader and Cabinet Minister Roy Hattersley put his finger on the deep-seated nature of the problem with his succinct indictment of Labour's 2010 general election defeat: 'The Party not only failed to set out a clear and coherent idea of what it proposed to do. It was not even sure about the purpose of its existence.'

Although in 2015 Labour won 740,000 more votes, its 30 per cent share of the votes cast fell well short of the 43 per cent in its 1997 landslide. Over four million votes had gone missing, the great majority under Tony Blair by 2005.

Underlying the decline of Europe's social democratic parties has been a striking loss of self-confidence in projecting a serious alternative to the right and its neoliberal ideology. Unable or unwilling to adopt a distinct anti-austerity stance, they have been settling for second best by offering a pale imitation of right-wing economic policies, and suffering a serious loss of support with voters looking elsewhere for hope of a better future.

In Britain this meant Labour fighting the 2015 election on a vague call for 'sensible cuts' in public spending. That, it was claimed, would restore Labour's lost credibility on economic policy by making the Party appear more 'responsible' in the eyes of an electorate that supposedly attributed big budget deficits to alleged Labour 'overspending' before the 2008 global financial crisis. Although it offered only a milder version of Conservative austerity, it was a stance widely backed, if not in detail then in general, by a range of Labour opinion including leading MPs, Fabians and *Progress* supporters.

Paradoxically its principal architect, the then Labour Shadow Chancellor Ed Balls had argued something rather different in his August 2010 Bloomberg lecture. That was when he explained why, by trying to force the pace of deficit reduction, Tory Chancellor George Osborne risked stalling the engine of growth and trapping the UK economy in a slow growth/no growth equilibrium that could last for years. Which is what duly happened.Osborne's austerity first halted Labour's carefully nurtured growth following the global banking crisis and the ensuing recession, then caused the recovery to stall for fully three years. Growth took off for just a year before dropping back as the economy lost momentum. UK growth in 2015 was slower than in 2014 and is forecast to be slower still in 2016. The result? Osborne fell behind schedule on his debt targets and went significantly over-budget on borrowing where he became a serial offender.

In the financial year 2015–16 he delivered a £76 billion borrowing figure – exceeding the figure forecast by Chancellor Alistair Darling in his final Labour budget in March 2010 when he planned to bring down Britain's budget deficit over the following Parliament to £74 billion in 2014–15.

Yet it was precisely Labour's £74 billion level of planned borrowing that the new Tory Chancellor condemned when he took over at the Treasury. It would take Britain close to 'the brink of bankruptcy', he fulminated, insisting Labour could not be trusted. Instead he replaced it in June 2010 with new tougher targets, halving Labour's planned borrowing in 2014–15 from £74 billion to £37 billion and setting himself a tight borrowing target of £20 billion for 2015–16.

Both those targets were missed by a mile. By March 2016 debt was £275 billion above Osborne's target and the 2015–16 budget deficit was £56 billion higher than he had planned in 2010. So much for the credibility of his 'long term economic plan'. After the Brexit referendum on 23 June 2016, with the economy rocky, even Osborne shamelessly abandoned his destructively unattainable plan for a budget surplus by 2020.

That, however, did not stop him continuing to play the Greece card which robbed his faint-hearted critics of their resolve just as effectively as kryptonite robbed Superman of his strength. They were afraid to back an alternative to austerity after swallowing the Osborne line that to do so would trigger inflation or lose confidence in the bond markets, raising the risk of being unable to borrow except at sky high interest rates or, like Greece, not being able to borrow at all – propaganda simply swallowed by spineless uncritical British newspapers and broadcasters, which made challenging it difficult for politicians.

Yet all the Chancellor's scaremongering about Britain becoming another Greece proved to be nonsense. Just like under Labour Chancellor Darling even during the banking crisis, Britain has had no problem financing its budget deficit and the yield on UK government debt dropped to an all-time low of 1.22 per cent in February 2016. The Chancellor kept crying wolf while the bond market kept behaving more like Britain's best friend.

From consensus to financial crisis

Fifty years after Ben Tillett's outburst, Tony Crosland in his seminal book, *The Future of Socialism*,[3] pointed out that the 1945–51 Labour government had overcome severe postwar austerity to carry out a social revolution that exceeded even the most optimistic expectations of 1930s radicals such as GDH Cole and Evan Durbin. What is more, Crosland was confident that the Conservative Party had accepted the postwar social framework.

A political consensus saw cross-party support for a welfare state inspired by Beveridge, full employment policies based on Keynes, and tax and spending measures that encouraged greater equality and fewer class differences. That consensus lasted until the advent of Thatcherism when the neoliberal challenge to the hegemony of social democratic ideas began – and from which we are still suffering today. Since 1980 neoliberals have disputed the role of the state acting on behalf of society in support of the public interest. Instead, they denigrate collective action and back market forces and self-reliance. Of course social democrats, or democratic socialists, respect the productive power of markets. We want to harness market forces to the promotion of the common good. When Brad DeLong in 2014 compared GDP per head in east European centrally-planned economies with that in matched west European market-based economies before the fall of the iron curtain, he found that productivity in the soviet bloc states was less than 20 per cent that of the market-based economies. Only a dogmatist would ignore such evidence.[4]

Social democrats, however, also know that markets require regulation because they often fail, sometimes spectacularly so, as in 2008 when a global financial crisis brought the entire economic system to the brink of complete collapse. Progressive economic management requires a deft balance between free-market forces and responsible state intervention. As JK Galbraith explained in *The Great Crash*, we are conservatives who seek antidotes to the suicidal tendencies of the capitalist system and are therefore dismissed as radicals.[5]

In retrospect, the 2007–08 global banking crisis showed that Labour had been blind to a threat of financial instability. Critically, we had allowed recklessly irresponsible bank lending to become a law unto itself, untroubled by a flawed system of financial regulation. In common with most other governments across the world, we had permitted market forces to have their head, and they had run away with us, as, like lemmings, the herd instinct took financial institutions right over the edge.

Today, the casino side of banking still poses a deadly threat to economic stability, with bankers facing the same temptation to take reckless risks in the belief that the taxpayer will step in to save them when things go wrong again. As they surely will, because free-market systems are inherently unstable and financial markets are prone to periodic failure. Except that next time the banks may become too big to save. It is all very well saying, as the IMF did in 2014, that across the advanced economies the net cost of rescuing the banks was at most 3 per cent of GDP, once the crisis had passed and government equity stakes in bailed-out banks had been recovered. But at the peak of the crisis the total value of support from governments and central banks by injecting capital, providing liquidity and guaranteeing liabilities, was equivalent to 74 per cent of UK GDP and overall 25 per cent of world GDP.

Former IMF chief economist Simon Johnson has summed up the situation: 'We are nearing the end of our fiscal and monetary ability to bail out the system. We are steadily becoming vulnerable to disaster on an epic scale.'[6] The left should be insisting upon stricter rules for all financial institutions, including the shadow banking sector of private equity outfits and hedge funds, so that the public interest becomes paramount.

Neoliberalism ought to be lying in pieces, fit only for the rubbish bin of history. The global financial crisis that threatened to plunge the world economy into a second great depression and from which after eight long years European economies are still only slowly recovering, ought never to have happened according to the efficient markets hypothesis. Neoliberal theory says that the financial system is self-correcting. Sudden shocks on the scale of the 2008 banking crisis ought not to occur, and if they do the system is supposed to correct itself quickly with no need for significant state intervention. But the scale of the state rescue of the financial system – in the UK alone £133 billion in cash outlays and a potential cost including government guarantees of over £1,100 billion – surely shattered any myth about a financial system with self-stabilising properties.

Reviving the role of the state

Europe's social democrats need to regain their economic self-assurance. The place to start is by recognising the success of Keynesian economics in dealing with the threat of a second great depression triggered by the global financial crisis. In the short term adopting a big fiscal stimulus to reverse the current slowdown, get the economy growing again, and growing quickly, should be our top priority.

Some colleagues say that 'Labour's abandonment of fiscal conservatism has turned off swing voters' and instead propose combining 'economic radicalism with fiscal prudence', as Tristram Hunt MP put it in May 2016.[7] But it is on the growth rate of the economy that budget deficits and the debt burden ultimately depend. How fast the economy grows before 2020 is key to deciding what will happen to Britain's deficit and the debt-to-GDP ratio by the next election. Promoting faster growth, not endless austerity, is the surest route to stable public finances.

Yet even 2016 IMF research showing that 'Instead of delivering growth, some neoliberal policies have increased inequality, in turn jeopardising durable expansion' is unlikely to stem the constant clamour for neoliberal austerity.[8]

Instead, Europe's centre-left parties should be arguing for the rate of deficit reduction to be linked to the pace of economic recovery and taking vigorous fiscal action to promote faster growth. In Britain that could mean an immediate £30 billion boost to public investment for each of the next two years aimed at housebuilding, infrastructure, education and skills and low carbon investment.

Looking further ahead, longer life expectancy and increasing demand for what the American management writer Peter Drucker termed 'knowledge workers' means an *expanding* role for the state in education, pensions and health services, especially elderly care.[9] Neoliberals' attempts to shrink the role of the state are taking society in entirely the wrong direction. Social democrats must stop acquiescing in such mistaken strategies and renew the case for a balance between private enterprise and public provision. As Jacob Hacker and Paul Pierson say in their 2016 study of the part played by government in helping advanced societies to flourish: 'The mixed economy remains a spectacular achievement…By combining the power of markets with a strong dose of public authority, we achieved unprecedented prosperity'.[10]

Second, everyone outside the financial system now realises that light-touch regulation of the banks was a blunder. Insiders like former Governor of the Bank of England Lord King and IMF boss Christine Lagarde warn that another financial crisis cannot be ruled out. Breaking up the big banks, to separate retail banking from investment banking, with taxpayers guaranteeing only the socially essential parts such as payment systems and customers' deposits – and not the risky casino side – is essential to prevent another financial collapse. Uncertain financial firewalls are not tough enough.

Third, growing inequality must be reversed by social democratic policies or the parliamentary left will have forfeited any right to renewed popular support. Research in 2015 showed that there had been no rise in the real wages of working and lower-middle class Americans since the late 1970s; indeed the level was actually lower than in the late 1960s and early 1970s. No wonder that in 2016 Donald Trump's ugly rightist populism found a ready response, including among that key former Democrat constituency of white working-class Americans. No wonder the left's Senator Bernie Sanders ran the establishment Democrat Hillary Clinton's brand of humane neoliberalism uncomfortably close. As middle and lower America lost out, and inequality widened hugely, ordinary citizens have rebelled.

Centrist US economic commentator Rana Foroohar's 2016 book, *Makers and Takers: The Rise of Finance and the Fall of American Business*,[1] argued that Adam Smith's vision of market capitalism had broken.

Markets, she showed, no longer supported the economy and delivered only divisive and slower than normal growth, where the very rich got richer and the rest trailed behind. 'Market capitalism was set up to funnel worker savings into new businesses via the financial system. But only 15 per cent of the capital in financial institutions today goes toward that goal – the rest exists in a closed loop of trading and speculation.' She added: 'In the US, finance doubled in size since the 1970s, and now makes up 7 per cent of the economy and takes a quarter of all corporate profits, more than double what it did back then. Yet it creates only 4 per cent of all jobs. Similar figures hold true for the UK.'

Adair Turner, former Chairman of Britain's Financial Services Authority, confirms the view that much financial activity is 'socially useless' in his 2016 book *Between Debt and the Devil*. He argues that the vast majority of bank lending in advanced economies 'does not support new business investment but instead funds either increased consumption or the purchase of already existing assets, in particular real estate and the urban land on which it sits'. [12]

Unless social democracy provides an alternative to such systemic neoliberal failure, we will not recover the ground lost, either in Britain or across the world. My 2015 book, *Back to the Future of Socialism*, lays out both an evidence-based, credible alternative and a critique of the poverty of neoliberalism. [13]

Europe: refugees and austerity

In Europe the refugee crisis coming on top of large-scale migration has been made even more unpopular by austerity policies since 2008. Public anger about immigration is a result of much deeper political alienation at the failure of Europe's governments to deliver a better, more secure economic future.

For 30 years after the Second World War, right across Europe, Keynesian full employment measures combined with welfare state policies delivered economic and social stability, promoting the necessary investment and faster economic growth as well as more just, more equal societies and fewer class differences.

For nearly four decades now, however, we have suffered from neoliberal ideology – that is to say a small-government ideology favouring market forces wherever possible and tolerating state regulation only where absolutely necessary.

In *Capital in the Twenty-First Century* Thomas Piketty in 2014 showed that since neoliberalism was adopted from around 1980, capitalism has reverted to type with an inbuilt tendency to generate shocking degrees of wealth and income inequality, which he predicts will continue throughout this century without changes in government policy.[14]

This in turn has caused a revolt against European political elites, left and right, as is shown by:

- in Britain, the 2016 European referendum, popular anger at the political class, with immigration especially noxious among working-class citizens who felt that they had been left behind;
- in Scotland, the strength of the separatists in the 2014 Scottish referendum, the 2015 general election and the 2016 Scottish Parliament election; in England, the rise of the United Kingdom Independence Party (UKIP); and in Britain's Labour Party in 2015 a new populist leader with a huge mandate from its members;
- in Spain, the rise of Podemos and Ciudadanos, and pressure for Catalonia to separate;
- in France, the rise of the Front National which has attracted working-class voters who used to vote Communist or Socialist;
- in Greece, Golden Dawn on the fascist right and Syriza on the populist left;
- in Germany, Denmark and Hungary the rise of far-right parties;
- in Austria, a near victory for the far-right candidate in the 2016 Presidential elections, with the previously strong social democrats trailing miserably behind;
- in Poland, new right-wing government restrictions on the judiciary, media and civil service, triggering a formal European Union investigation;

- in even social democratic Sweden, its general election in September 2014 saw the far right more than double support to 13 per cent and come third;
- in many countries, migrants have become the scapegoat, the problem in Britain politically toxic, even though their youth and skills – 40 per cent of the first huge tide of Syrian refugees in 2015 were graduates – can boost our ageing societies across Europe.

By supporting moderate austerity, Europe's parliamentary parties of the left (such as in Greece PASOK and in Spain PSOE) have failed to offer an alternative economic agenda and so have haemorrhaged support to populist parties of the left and right.

Greece is the most vivid example of how austerity, far from solving a difficult debt problem, can make it worse. After the first EU programme of austerity Greek national debt jumped by one third to over 170 per cent. GDP dropped by over 25 per cent, unemployment reached 26 per cent, youth unemployment soared above 50 per cent, and Greek wages fell by more than 30 per cent.

The second austerity programme imposed upon Greece will make it even worse, with even the IMF agreeing that there is no chance of Greece repaying its loans and reducing its debt.

Here the irony is Germany – with Willy Brandt's Social Democrats sharing government – imposing on Greece the kind of austerity it suffered under the Treaty of Versailles after the First World War, with the appalling economic and political consequences which that produced.

Meanwhile the Greek islands were being flooded with desperate refugees, with the United Nations announcing at the end of October 2015 that over half a million had entered the country over the year. One proposal at the height of the crisis to expel Greece from the Schengen open borders zone would have trapped many more thousands of refugees inside a country with borders of 14,000 kilometres (the longest in Europe).

Although an abandonment of neoliberalism and a reversion to Keynesian policies across Europe will not make the sources of conflict in North Africa and the Middle East, and therefore the refugee crisis, go away, that would help manage it much more effectively.

Growth is the key

Achieving faster growth in the medium and longer term means acting on the lesson learned late in the life of the last Labour government and adopting an active industrial strategy. In her book, *The Entrepreneurial State*, Mariana Mazzucato has cited dozens of examples from American, South Korean, Taiwanese and German experience, of where the state has been the source of innovation, prompting technological advance in areas like aviation, the internet, biotechnology and green technology.[15]

Also, Britain's small and medium-sized businesses need a British investment bank to provide the long-term lending and modest amounts of equity capital that small and medium-sized enterprises (SMEs) in Germany enjoy from the state-owned development bank Kreditanstalt für Wiederaufbau (KfW). Nicholas Tott's 2013 report for the Labour Party pointed out that the UK is the only member of the G8 not to have a dedicated institution dealing with SME financing issues. We have nothing to compare with the KfW or the Small Business Administration in the US.[16]

Such a British investment bank could also help to finance investment in infrastructure, including accelerating investment in housing and in low-carbon innovation by attracting funding from pension funds and insurance companies, because the latter need to acquire long-term assets to match their long-term liabilities. An initiative like this would fit with what radical thinkers such as Noah Smith in the US calls 'New Industrialism': 'an approach to economic policy that respects the power of the private sector but isn't afraid of an activist government'.[17]

Mixed progress in a mixed economy

In ten years of government leading up to the global financial crisis, Labour made mixed progress towards the five basic aspirations which

Tony Crosland in 1956 saw as the core socialist values. These values were:

- a protest against poverty;
- a concern for social welfare and the interests of the disadvantaged in particular;
- a belief in greater equality and a classless society;
- support for cooperation and fraternity over competition and self-interest;
- a protest against capitalism's tendency towards mass unemployment.

In thirteen years we cut child and pensioner poverty and alleviated social distress by spending more on public services.

We helped the disadvantaged in particular by improving welfare benefits while reducing the share of Britain's expanding GDP spent on social security.

We achieved record levels of employment.

Inequality continued to worsen, however, with the real incomes of many on middle incomes growing only slowly if at all. Labour never acknowledged that UK taxes are broadly proportional not progressive, and we remained reticent in public about redistribution.

Not surprisingly, because New Labour extolled the neoliberal virtues of competition, self-assertion and entrepreneurialism rather than cooperation, fellowship and public service became the norm.

In *The Future of Socialism*, Crosland saw economic growth as key to realising all five aims. What made progress possible over the decade 1997 to 2007 was that the UK economy grew steadily, averaging 3 per cent per year. Crosland saw the state playing a pivotal role in using collective power to promote both individual rights and the common good. That was what the last Labour government did and it should be Labour's philosophy in the future.

Notwithstanding its neoliberal flirtations, the last Labour government showed what social democracy can deliver. Labour took office in 1997 committed to standing by the Tories' public spending plans for the next two years. Our pledge card had promised to set tough rules for government spending and borrowing. Within days of taking over at the Treasury in 1997 Gordon Brown launched an immediate comprehensive public spending review. The results of that review appeared on Bastille Day, 14 July 1998. Many Party members hoped it would prove to be Labour's get out of jail free card for public spending. But they had to remain patient for some while yet. As promised, Labour kept public spending in check.

Despite these frustrations with our initial restraint, it proved to be the prelude to years of record investment in the public services.

- Over the years 1997 to 2010 spending on public services increased by an average of 4.4 per cent a year in real terms compared to the 0.7 per cent a year average rise that the Tories delivered from 1979 to 1997, largely due to increased spending on the NHS, education and transport.
- After 2000–01 public investment increased especially sharply, reaching in 2008–09 a share of national income not seen since the late 1970s. It was nearly five times the share of 1996–97.
- According to Office for National Statistics estimates, public services improved considerably over the period 1997 to 2007, with measured outputs suggesting a one third increase in the quantity and quality of public services.

At the same time – and contrary to the big deceit embedded in the British public's mind by the Tories and a compliant British media – Labour management of the public finances was prudent. The national debt was reduced, and so was the deficit, from levels inherited in 1997. Before the global banking crisis triggered sky-high levels of debt and borrowing, these were also low by international standards. Yet a myth has been created that Labour 'spent too much'. We did not.

Labour's extra spending, largely financed by a record ten years of growth, however, is why NHS waiting times and waiting lists, school class sizes and crime all came down. It paid for 70,000 more nurses and 40,000 more doctors in England alone, and supplied over 100 new hospitals and 650 one-stop primary care centres. It allowed 40,000 more teachers and 115,000 more teaching assistants to be recruited and 3,000 Sure Start children's centres to be opened. It provided 15,000 more police officers and 16,000 new community support officers. At root it is why Labour left the NHS in 2010 with the highest ever levels of public satisfaction. Today, however, Britain still has nearly three million children, more than six million adults of working age, and two million pensioners living in poverty; five million people on social housing waiting lists; and 17 million citizens living with a long-term health condition (such as a heart condition, diabetes or asthma).

Where both a fast-ageing society and a chronic housing shortage demand more not less government, the British state continues to be shrunk by a dogmatic neoliberal mission. Our public services are being cut and outsourced. Job insecurity and low pay are rife. Occupational pensions are expiring. Skills lag abysmally. Productivity is embarrassingly low and the trade deficit both embarrassingly and historically high.

All this cries out for a newly resurgent social democracy or democratic socialism. But will Labour and our sister parties in Europe respond, or will we be eclipsed?

Notes

[1] Peter Hain is grateful for the assistance of Phil Wyatt in writing this Foreword.

[2] B. Tillett, *Is the Parliamentary Labour Party a Failure?* (London: Twentieth Century Press, 1909).

[3] C.A.R. Crosland, *The Future of Socialism* (London: Cape, 1956).

[4] B. DeLong, 'Lecture notes for economics 2', 29 January 2014, University of California at Berkeley.

[5] J.K. Galbraith, *The Great Crash: 1929* (London: Hamilton, 1955).

[6] P. Boone and S. Johnson, 'Will the politics of global moral hazard sink us again?', in *The Future of Finance – The LSE Report* (London: LSE, 2010) p 272.

[7] T. Hunt, 'Labour needs a positive path out of political irrelevance', *Financial Times*, 9 May 2016.

[8] www.imf.org/external/pubs/ft/fandd/2016/06/ostry.htm.

[9] P. Drucker, *The Landmarks of Tomorrow* (New York: Harper and Row, 1959).

[10] J.S. Hacker and P. Pierson, *American Amnesia* (New York: Simon and Schuster, 2016) p 337.

[11] R. Foroorah, *Makers and Takers: The Rise of Finance and the Fall of American Business* (London: Crown Business, 2016).

[12] A. Turner, *Between Debt and the Devil* (Princeton, NJ: Princeton University Press, 2016).

[13] P. Hain, *Back to the Future of Socialism* (Bristol: Policy, 2015).

[14] T. Picketty, *Capital in the Twenty-first Century* (Cambridge, MA: Harvard University Press, 2014).

[15] M. Mazzucato, *The Entrepreneurial State* (London: Anthem Press, 2013).

[16] N. Tott, 'The case for a British investment bank' (London: Labour Party, 2012).

[17] www.bloomberg.com/view/articles/2016-05-26/finding-better-ideas-to-rebuild-america.

Introduction[1]

Kevin Hickson

Labour's General Election defeat in 2015 has arguably highlighted the crisis of social democracy in Britain, just as it struggles elsewhere to gain credibility and popular support. The election defeat followed five years of unpopular government, with leaders who were deemed out of touch and uncaring and policies which had undermined the social fabric of the United Kingdom in the pursuit of 'austerity'. Some may argue that this defeat was down to an unfortunate combination of factors including the rise of Scottish Nationalism, the loss of Liberal Democrat seats which benefited the Tories in the south and the rise of the United Kingdom Independence Party (UKIP). This is undoubtedly true, but to argue that Labour doesn't need to change as these unfortunate set of factors should be avoided in future and because the Conservative divisions were exposed in the EU Referendum campaign would be complacent. Despite the widening inequality and increased poverty of the years of Coalition government the Tories were still returned with a majority and the Labour Party is now itself fundamentally divided with little serious ideological reflection and new ideas since the 1990s.[2] There was also a clear disconnect between the Labour Party establishment and Labour voters in its heartland areas over the EU. At the time of writing Labour appears to be struggling to find a new agenda post-Brexit.

Political parties do not need to win the battle of ideas in order to win elections. They may win them through the personal standing of their

Leader, the conspiring of events, or simply the feeling that it is time for a change. However, they can only create lasting policy legacies if they have won the battle of ideas. Parties can rarely rethink fundamentally when they are in power as the pressures of time and the speed of events ensure that they lack the opportunity for reflection. They must therefore do so out of power. Even then a political party that wins an election with a clear programme of reform may be blown off course as unexpected events occur for which the ideological reconfiguration out of power did not prepare them, something which is truer the longer a party is in power. Hence, the Conservative government prior to 1997 and the Labour government prior to 2010 had both appeared to have run out of steam some years before their eventual demise.

The extent to which New Labour was dominant is open to debate.[3] Clearly they were dominant electorally winning a landslide election victory in 1997 and 2001 and a reduced, but still sizeable, majority in 2005. This was the first time Labour had won a full second term, let alone a third. But even here the state of the Conservatives after 1997 should be noted. Badly divided over Europe and rocked by the sleaze and corruption that dogged the tail end of the Major government, the Tories twice rejected leadership candidates who on all objective criteria would have been more effective than the triumphant candidates. It was only after 2005 that the traditional Conservative statecraft of winning elections was restored with 'modernisation' under David Cameron.

New Labour left a clear policy legacy, but the extent to which it marked the revival of social democracy is debateable. The years between 1997 and 2010 witnessed significant policy developments including the National Minimum Wage, the adoption of the Social Chapter of the Maastricht Treaty, redistribution of income and record levels of spending on health and education. However, the gap between rich and poor widened, privatisation of state-owned assets and marketisation of public services continued. There was little attempt to alter the balance of power in the workplace which had swung heavily in favour of employers under Thatcher and Major and the economy remained heavily skewed towards finance capitalism, which was lightly regulated until the banking crisis. If there was a revival of social democratic policies – and certainly the above list highlights a number of achievements which would never have happened if the Conservatives had remained in office – then it was within the broad parameters of a neoliberal economic framework created by the previous Conservative governments and facilitated by the increased internationalisation of economic activity.

Certainly the last Labour government left a sense of disappointment (and outright anger over the war in Iraq). Of the 2010 leadership candidates, David Miliband suffered by being seen as the 'continuity' candidate. The successor, his younger brother Ed, was seen as offering more change and a subtle move to the left. His defeat in the 2015 General Election marked a further outpouring of disappointment and, in hindsight, the election of Jeremy Corbyn should not be seen as a surprise. Labour governments had always failed to live up to the aspirations of the activists, even the 1945–51 governments, which left-wing critics argued had simply sought to revive capitalism rather than implement socialism and was too close to the United States. The subsequent Labour governments of 1964–70 and 1974–79 were again criticised by those on the left as 'managing capitalism' and betraying the wishes of the grassroots of the Party, something that led to the rise of the Labour left in the early 1980s with their 'Alternative Economic Strategy' and plans to 'democratise' the Party. Moreover, the new electoral system which allowed members of the public to pay £3 to become a registered supporter with immediate voting rights helped the cause of the left-wing candidate in the 2015 leadership election.

The extent to which the Party now has a clear purpose, however, is still open to debate. It is certainly true that Labour has its most left-wing Leader since Michael Foot, George Lansbury or perhaps ever. However, his election has split the Party with the majority of MPs opposed to the Leader whom they had had thrust upon them and the majority of members supporting the new Leader, a tension that reached its peak in the immediate aftermath of the decision to leave the EU with the mass resignations from Corbyn's Shadow Cabinet and subsequent leadership challenge.

In such a fevered environment most publications outlining possible courses of action for the Labour Party are factional and, often intentionally, supportive of, or hostile to, the Leader. They are frequently written by sectional organisations within the Labour Party and wider movement and deal with immediate issues.

The aim here is not to repeat that much trodden path. Instead, we seek to go back to the basic values of the Labour Party and examine how they can be revised in light of recent domestic and international changes and what policies flow from them. These policies must be both credible and radical and I return to these themes in the Conclusion to this volume.

Structure of the book

Each author was given considerable autonomy over what they wrote and the arguments they chose to make. The book has no overall objectives other than to provoke discussion and debate over the most effective ways in which social democracy can be revived in Britain.

However, in order to give some structure to the book authors were requested to examine three questions.

- What have been the main ways in which British socialists have addressed these concepts in the past?
- What is the contemporary socialist/social democratic case for these principles?
- In broad terms what policy implications follow from this new philosophical case?

The first question was intended to provide a brief historical and/or theoretical contextualisation for the majority of the discussion, which would focus on the second and third questions. The second question required a more philosophical discussion and the response to the final question would need to be more applied and policy focused.

The distinction between the underlying philosophy and policy is a well trodden approach to social democracy in Britain. This distinction between ends and means was a mainstay of Revisionism in the 1950s, especially in the work of Tony Crosland.[4] Ends relates to the underlying ethical foundations and the means to the policies developed to bring those to fruition. For the Revisionists the ends/means distinction was clear cut. Nationalisation, long seen as an objective of socialism for the Labour left was relegated in importance to a means – one way, and not even an important one, of achieving the end goal of equality. However, others have more recently sought to show that the relationship between ends and means is more complex.[5] Certain policies are essential means to achieve given socialist objectives. For instance, greater equality of income and wealth would be impossible to achieve without progressive taxation. Equally, the end goal of socialism may differ from socialist to socialist. Equality was presented as an end goal by 1950s Revisionists but to the next generation equality was an instrumental value for the attainment of true liberty.[6] Others would argue that community ought to be a more foundational value for social democracy than liberty. These are huge questions for social democrats and space here does not permit an answer to them – indeed a final, definite answer may not be possible. The ends and means of social democracy differ over time.

One further preliminary point needs discussion here. The terminology of socialism and social democracy. I have used these terms interchangeably and in so doing have followed the mainstream approach within the history of the Labour Party. In the early years social democracy was the ideological term used by the more radical elements in the Party, the Social Democratic Federation. In the 1980s, even Labour moderates preferred to use the term socialism (usually prefixed with 'Democratic') to distinguish their position from the more centrist ideology of the Social Democratic Party. Before that, even some moderates had used the term 'democratic socialism' in preference to 'social democracy', which was seen as more continental. However, for most of the time the terms social democracy and democratic socialism have been used interchangeably. For instance Tony Crosland's last book, *Socialism Now* contains a piece with that name and another entitled 'Social Democracy in Britain'.[7] Some authors in this volume prefer to use the term social democracy and others socialism. In essence we mean the same thing, a commitment to a set of recognisably left-of-centre ethical values which are to be implemented through the democratic process. Hence, it differs from both the revolutionary road to socialism advocated by those further to the left and the ideas of the free market advocated by the right.

The Social Democrat Philosophy Group

It was while staying with my good friends Matt and Claire Beech, in the wee small hours of 2 February 2010, that Matt first raised the idea of a new discussion forum of centre-left academics. After attending that year's Centre for British Politics' Norton Lecture at the University of Hull given by Raymond Plant, a late night discussion turned to the future of the Labour Party. It was fairly clear by that point that the Labour government was running out of steam. The consensus was that the Party needed fresh thinking and a clear social democratic prospectus. But, like most Labour supporters, we were pessimistic about the Party's chances in the forthcoming General Election. That evening Raymond Plant, who had been the supervisor for both of our PhDs at the University of Southampton, suggested that it was time to pass the baton to the next generation. He had been instrumental in the Socialist Philosophy Group which had developed fresh thinking which had helped the modernisation of the Labour Party under Neil Kinnock and Roy Hattersley.

After an initial planning meeting the Social Democrat Philosophy Group held its inaugural meeting in Committee Room 3a of the House of Lords on 22 July 2010 in the company of Lord Parekh. Since then, meetings have been held in Oxford, Birmingham, Liverpool and Nottingham where colleagues have presented papers and this book represents the fruits of their labour.

The Social Democrat Philosophy Group is intellectually diverse and does not seek to represent a specific school of Labour thought, Party faction or particular individual politician. The ties that bind the Group are our support for Labour; our belief in social justice; and our determination to aid in the revision of Labour ideas and policies so to challenge the politics of austerity which has defined British politics since 2010. The views expressed in each chapter are the views of the individual author, just as those opinions expressed in this Introduction and the Conclusion are the views of the Editor and should not be seen as a corporate view.

Acknowledgements

I would like to thank the contributors who gave their time to write their chapters when they had many other commitments in terms of teaching, marking and writing.

I am especially pleased that Peter Hain agreed to write the Foreword. I have long been an admirer. He has a distinguished past as an anti-Apartheid campaigner, was a very able Minister especially in rescuing the peace process in Northern Ireland and has written one of the very few original works on British socialism in recent years, *Back to the Future of Socialism*.[8]

We have received generous support from the editorial staff at Policy Press.

Finally, we are grateful to anyone who reads this book. You may or may not agree with some or all of the ideas expressed within it, but if we provoke discussion and debate over the future direction of the Labour Party then we have done what we set out to do.

Notes

[1] I am very grateful to Matt Beech for comments on this piece, my own chapter on Political Economy and the Conclusion.

[2] The one exception to this was the debate inspired by 'Blue Labour' and the response from orthodox social democrats. See R. Hattersley and K. Hickson 'In praise of social democracy' and the various responses to it in *The Political Quarterly* 83/1 (2012), pp 5–19.

[3] See the opening and closing chapters of M. Beech and S. Lee (eds) *Ten Years of New Labour* (Basingstoke: Palgrave, 2008) by the editors.

[4] C.A.R. Crosland, *The Future of Socialism* (London: Cape, 1956).

[5]   See R. Plant 'Ends, means and political identity' in R. Plant, M. Beech and K. Hickson (eds) *The Struggle for Labour's Soul* (London: Routledge, 2005).
[6]   See R. Hattersley, *Choose Freedom* (London: Michael Joseph, 1987).
[7]   C.A.R. Crosland, S*ocialism Now* (London: Cape, 1974).
[8]   P. Hain, *Back to the Future of Socialism* (Bristol: Policy, 2015).

ONE

Political economy

Kevin Hickson

'The entire discourse justifying the scale of public spending austerity is manufactured to serve the ideological end of shrinking the state.' Will Hutton[1]

Throughout a long period of Opposition the Labour Party strove to regain a reputation for economic credibility that was lost in the 'Winter of Discontent' in 1978–79. Ironically, Labour was returned to power when the economy under John Major and Kenneth Clarke was improving but when the Party had lost trust among the public for the forced and costly withdrawal from the European Exchange Rate Mechanism in September 1992. Throughout the ten years of Tony Blair's Premiership and with Gordon Brown at the Treasury the economy continued to expand. The succession of Brown as Prime Minister was assured as a result of his reputation as an economic manager but was immediately undermined by the banking crisis of 2007. The most effective piece of political rhetoric since then has been that the Conservatives are sorting out 'Labour's economic mess' and even by 2015 Labour still lagged behind on 'economic competence', a key factor which explains the Party's defeat at the last general election.

The point of this very brief history is that economic performance, as in the policies of the government of the day, and economic competence, as in the way in which the policies of governments are judged by the public, very often differ. Although there are those on the right who continue to believe that Mrs Thatcher saved Britain, this can only be maintained by neglecting the fact that there were two deep recessions under the Conservatives between 1979 and 1997, that unemployment increased and remained high throughout the 1980s and that growth was slower than in the postwar era which she denounced as a period of decline. Similarly, the idea that the economic crisis of 2007 was the fault of too much government – and particularly too much government spending – can only be sustained by ignoring the overwhelming body of evidence. Nevertheless, these myths are maintained and any social democratic political economy needs to deal both with economic reality and economic perception.

The task of this chapter – vital if Labour is to regain power – is to set out what an alternative political economy would look like. This political economy needs to be radical, in the sense of being clearly distinct from the prevailing neoliberal orthodoxy and credible, in the sense of addressing public perceptions. It will begin by examining the relationship between ideas and economic policy, the fundamental nature of the British economy and the ways in which Labour struggled to counter the austerity narrative between 2010 and 2015, before outlining a broad policy framework on which Labour can further develop as we approach the next general election. Regaining economic competence is a necessary, although not a sufficient, condition for a winning electoral strategy.

Ideology and economic policy

In his unfinished work, *A History of Economic Analysis,* Joseph Schumpeter drew a distinction between political economy and economic analysis.[2] Political economy was concerned with the normative assumptions about the ways in which the economy should be organised and the goals of economic policy. It was inseparable from ideology and therefore was not the remit of expert economists. Economic analysis is concerned with the rational application of certain policy tools and techniques to address certain economic problems. Traditionally these problems were unemployment, inflation, growth and the terms of international trade. The nature of these problems and their relative importance would change over time and addressing them would be an empirical matter depending on the conditions at a particular time. Freed from normative assumptions, economic science could develop as an objective academic discipline.

Traditionally, the role of ideas in economic policy was deemed important whether that be in the classical political economy of Adam Smith and David Ricardo or Marxian political economy. However, the neoclassical turn in economic analysis sought to strip out any ethical or ideological concerns and turn economics into a rational scientific discipline, and so from that point the study of economics frequently turned on the formulation and application of models and statistical analyses. Positive economics was detached from normative economics.

This self-limiting approach ignored the fact that economic judgements cannot be separated from political ones. That is to say that economic theories are best understood as ideological. The prioritisation of economic goals – whether to favour full employment over price stability for instance – cannot be separated from notions of economic justice and class interest. If Marxian political economy is concerned with the promotion of proletarian interests then neoliberalism is concerned with the promotion of bourgeois interests. Keynesian economics is concerned with achieving a social consensus between competing class interests. From the perspective of Keynesians the postwar era marked a period of success in which full employment was maintained, the economy grew and the lives of working people improved. From the point of view of its critics – from the left and the right – the Keynesian era was one of stalemate in which the state propped up an ailing economy and Britain experienced relative economic decline.

The relevance of this for contemporary analysis is that since 1979 there has been a free-market economic counter-revolution inspired by the ideas of the likes of Friedrich von Hayek and Milton Friedman and implemented by governments of both political persuasions since 1979. Neoliberalism is now so firmly embedded, some would argue, that to use Margaret Thatcher's favourite acronym, TINA – there is no alternative. While David Cameron and George Osborne argued that there was no alternative to the austerity agenda because it is the only rational policy to employ given the scale of public sector debt, opponents would argue that austerity is an ideological choice and that therefore any concession to austerity is decamping on that neoliberal terrain. Against the agenda of neoliberal austerity there needs to be an alternative economic ideology posited. While few would argue for an overtly Marxian form of political economy following the collapse of the Eastern European model and economic reform in China, others would argue that Keynesian political economy – of varying degrees of radicalism – would provide a better model of political economy to neoliberal austerity.

Varieties of capitalism

From the perspective of the mid-twentieth century there was a fundamental choice of political economies between capitalism and communism. For radical/Marxist commentators the debates between Keynesians and monetarists was over alternative ways to operate the capitalist system and masked the more fundamental social divisions created by the existence of private property ownership. However, the collapse of Soviet Communism led some commentators, notably Francis Fukuyama,[3] to argue that we had experienced the end of history – understood as the fundamental clash of civilisations – with the triumph of western liberal capitalism. There was now no fundamental alternative to this model of political economy. This argument was reinforced by the idea of hyper-globalism – that we now lived in a 'borderless' world in which traditional national boundaries were no longer relevant as corporations had become more footloose.[4] The only viable option for national governments was now to create conditions in which it would become attractive for multinational firms to invest in one country rather than another through such things as low taxation and deregulation. Any other policy would be self-defeating as countries would lose out to competitor nations who did have more favourable policy frameworks for multinational corporations to maximise their profits. Both the 'end of history' and the hyper-globalisation thesis are examples of what Andrew Gamble has called the politics of fate – the idea that there are no fundamental choices to be made. Fate is the enemy of politics because politics is about making choices over the future direction of society.[5]

Other commentators pointed to the differences that existed between various models of capitalism with fundamentally different relationships between capital and labour, and differing roles for the state. The clearest attempt to outline this idea was that by Peter A Hall and David Soskice in *Varieties of Capitalism: The Institutional Foundations of Comparative Advantage* first published in 2001.[6] For Hall and Soskice there are several factors by which economies can be classified as 'liberal market economies' or 'coordinated market economies'. These two models were poles at opposite ends of the spectrum. No economy fitted purely into one or the other of these 'ideal types' but ranged somewhere along a continuous spectrum depending on several factors. First, industrial relations – the extent to which trade unions and corporations were integrated into the planning of economic decisions and the size of trade union membership. Second, vocational training and education – the extent to which workers have more transferable skills or skills specific to certain industries. Third, corporate governance and in particular the extent to which capital is offered on a short- or long-term basis. Next, the nature of relationships between businesses and whether they are marked more by cooperation or competition. Finally, whether relationships between employers and employees are more consensual or conflictual.

Liberal market economies such as the USA and the UK are marked more by weaker trade unions and more flexible labour markets, the promotion of transferable skills, short-term capital, competitive relationships between corporations and more adversarial relations between employers and labour. This model of capitalism is meant to offer a more dynamic model of economic activity underpinned by risk taking and entrepreneuralism according to its supporters and was promoted by the New Right in Britain and the United States in particular.

In contrast, coordinated market economies tend to have larger trade union memberships; regular consultation between employers, employees and government; the promotion of skills specific to certain employers meaning that workers tend to stay with the same firm for longer; the provision of longer-term capital which allows firms to invest in new technology; greater cooperation between corporations and between employers and employees. Such economies would include Germany, Austria, Japan and Sweden. According to advocates of this model, the mode of economic organisation allows for greater economic stability, a larger state and the provision of higher levels of welfare.

While Marxists may wish to argue that these are all forms of the same thing – namely capitalism – and are therefore still dependent on exploitation of workers and the profit motive, others would argue that the differences are fundamental. These differences – on the role of the state, the position of workers, the provision of credit and so on – are based on fundamentally opposing ideological perspectives, traditions and cultural identities.

One criticism of the 'varieties of capitalism' literature is that it is fundamentally conservative. Hall, in particular, had contributed in a major way to the historical school of institutionalism where national variations in political, social and economic organisation are based on long-held traditions. The model explains why there is continuity but cannot easily explain change. This point is relevant to our analysis here because some may argue, from a socialist or social democratic perspective, that the inherent injustice, instability and inequality that is seen in liberal market economies means that we should seek to simply emulate the achievements of coordinated market economies, but the emphasis on historical continuity would not allow for this. Coordinated market economies have developed in a certain way because of the national traditions of those countries whereas other countries have developed market liberal economies as a result of their peculiar historical development.

We should therefore be wary of suggesting that we can impose an alternative model of political economy in Britain ignoring the historical context. Nevertheless, there are, as we shall see, good reasons why those on the left and centre left would seek to move the British economy along the spectrum towards a more coordinated model of capitalism.

Before, I articulate practical measures that can be taken by the next Labour government to achieve this I wish first to examine further the ways in which Labour politicians have sought to respond to the politics of austerity.

The politics of austerity

Despite initially committing to maintaining Labour's spending plans in order to demonstrate their new, compassionate form of Conservatism, the Conservative Party quickly sought to blame the economic downturn on Labour's lax control of public expenditure. What was initially a crisis of markets and banking regulation was turned into a crisis of the state – from a crisis of banking regulation to a fiscal crisis. However, Labour's control of public spending had been tight in the early years leading to a budget surplus before 2000 and reasonable thereafter. In an attempt to show economic credibility and reassurance, Labour pledged not to alter Conservative spending plans for two years which in reality meant some spending cuts. After 1999 there was a significant increase in public expenditure but this was mainly from the fiscal dividends accrued from the expanding banking sector rather than from extra borrowing.

The response to the banking crisis was to expand credit so that banking liquidity was improved. The policy of 'quantitative easing' was designed to put back liquidity into the banking sector so that banks did not run out of cash. This had the effect of significantly increasing public sector debt but by the time Labour left office in 2010 there were some signs of economic growth and the Labour policy of repaying this additional borrowing meant that by 2010 the deficit was already being reduced. The policy was to further reduce the deficit, partly through cuts and partly through new growth, but at a slower rate than the Tories.

The Conservatives, however, announced that they would seek to reduce the deficit quicker and this had the effect of choking the growth that was beginning to emerge around 2010–11. The result has been that the public deficit and expenditure targets have continually been missed in successive budgets since 2010. Despite this, the Conservatives constantly repeated their belief that Labour had caused the deficit by increasing spending on social provision and that anyone who opposed the Tory cuts agenda, or who argued that the deficit should be repaid over a longer term, were dismissed as 'deficit deniers'. For some on the right, Osborne has not been sufficiently robust in cutting expenditure. The argument that the deficit should be reduced more through tax increases also met political opposition from the Conservatives apart from specific cases of tax avoidance where there was clear public opposition.

In light of this political situation, Labour has struggled to come up with a clear position since 2010. For some on the left of the Party there should be no cuts to public expenditure at all since this is an acceptance of the neoliberal agenda. For Jeremy Corbyn and his supporters, not only the last Labour governments but also the period of Opposition from 2010–15 was one of closet neoliberalism and much of Corbyn's success was due to the fact that he was resolutely opposed to austerity. However, the economic agenda which Corbyn articulated in his leadership campaign in 2015 appeared to his critics to be little more than a moral protest against austerity and that no credible alternative policy was put in place. Hence, since becoming Shadow Chancellor, John McDonnell has sought to propose an alternative economic strategy. The extent to which this will succeed will be seen. Success would need to be measured in terms of the outcome of the next general election, assuming he is still Shadow Chancellor by that time. This search for credibility has meant accepting fiscal rules similar to those made by Gordon Brown and Ed Balls, that there must be balance on the current account and borrowing must only be for investment. For some, this may be seen as a betrayal of the radical opposition to austerity on which Corbyn's leadership was acquired, whereas for others it marks a welcome acceptance of the need to regain economic credibility.

For others on the Labour right, the Party would not regain credibility without accepting some spending cuts.[7] In September 2010, Peter Kellner argued that, 'social democracy, as we have come to understand it, has become unaffordable'. Two months later, Blair's former senior advisor, Patrick Diamond, asserted that Labour must be 'much clearer on the specifics of spending cuts it will support if it is to restore fiscal credibility.' In 2012, policy analysts from pro-New Labour think tanks, Gavin Kelly and Nick Pearce stated that the outlook for public expenditure was 'unremittingly bleak'. The following year, Lord Liddle argued that social democratic parties across Europe needed to stick to rigid spending limits verified by independent budgetary authorities. In 2014, Diamond again warned that a future Labour government could not rely on economic growth to boost Treasury coffers. Defeat in the 2015 election encouraged some New Labourites to argue that this was proof of their pessimistic forecasts, that any deviation from 'Blairism' would be electoral suicide. However, for others this was a flawed strategy since the Conservatives, now in power on their own, would always outflank Labour when it came to austerity and so a credible alternative policy was still needed.

Towards a new model of political economy

The starting point for a credible alternative policy is the promotion of economic growth. Austerity is not a necessity. The economic crisis of 2008 was not a crisis of public spending. Before that date, borrowing had been stable. The increase in borrowing was a necessary measure to avert a recession becoming a depression. The failure was rather one of state regulation of financial capitalism, especially in Britain and the United States. In other words, it was too little government (in the form of regulation) rather than too much government (in the form of taxation, public spending and borrowing). Austerity is therefore an ideological agenda by neoliberal Conservatives who wished to build on the Thatcherite agenda of fiscal retrenchment.

The key to reducing the deficit is therefore not to cut spending, but to boost economic growth. Here the classic Keynesian policy of counter-cyclical fiscal expenditure once again becomes relevant. The government has a key role to play in boosting demand through more redistributive taxation and through capital investment.

Despite appearances, taxation in the UK is not progressive as Peter Hain has amply demonstrated in his book, *Back to the Future of Socialism*.[8] The richest individuals pay less taxation as a proportion of their income than the poorest and major corporations avoid taxation on a massive scale. In 2011–12, the richest 20 per cent of households paid 35.5 per cent of their gross income in taxes, compared with 36.6 per cent paid by the poorest 20 per cent. A more strictly progressive form of taxation – whereby the richer an individual is or the more profits a company makes the more taxes they pay – makes sense not only in terms of social justice but also economically.

Various proposals have been put forward to achieve these twin objectives. Hain advocates a seven-point programme of tax reforms.[9] First, he suggests reforms to inheritance tax so that it becomes more progressive. Second, a new higher rate of Council Tax, in effect a 'Mansion Tax' for properties in excess of £2 million. A financial transactions tax could be levied on sales and currency transactions, which could raise up to £20 billion. Moreover, reform of national insurance so that higher earners would pay the standard rate on all of their earnings and using this extra revenue to reduce the standard rate or raise the threshold so that those on lower earnings pay less. Higher earners would then pay a combined tax on their income of 62 per cent instead of the current 47 per cent (a higher rate of income tax as proposed in Labour's last manifesto plus the higher rate of national insurance). The change to national insurance would raise between £6 and £11 billion. Next, a higher rate of VAT could be levied on luxury goods. The congestion charge for central London could be rolled out to other major towns and cities. Finally, extra tax revenue could be raised on sport through taxing football transfer fees and TV broadcasting rights. Some would stress the need for further taxation on activities which have negative effects for the individual and the society such as betting taxes, and more taxes on alcohol and tobacco. Others would point to the failure of businesses to pay their fair share of Corporation Tax by moving their accounts overseas to a lower-tax regime and alternatives such as a sales tax have been floated so that profits are taxed at source.

The justification for austerity is often presented in terms of the household economy.[10] If individuals and families are spending more than they have coming in they need to economise. They may seek to take out loans but these will eventually need paying back with interest, making the need to cut back on their expenditure even more imperative. The same is said to be true for the government. Countries living beyond their means ultimately have to economise and borrowing to fund public expenditure irresponsibly passes on debt to future generations. However, the parallel between state expenditure and household expenditure is illusory. Governments have the capacity denied to households of printing money. They also have the capability to boost economic activity which then has the effect of reducing expenditure (through less demand for unemployment and other social security benefits) and increasing revenue (through taxation).

Therefore, public sector investment is a viable way to reduce the deficit, even if that means increasing it in the short term. This public spending can have other desirable effects such as investing in environmentally-sustainable technology and improving social capital. Hain outlines a viable programme of public sector investment, amounting to £30 billion per year for two years.[11] Although other reforms exist, the benefit of these proposals is not only that they are economically sensible but politically achievable. The first area where this new investment could be targeted is in terms of a new affordable housebuilding programme. In order to do this, there would be a need for development land to be brought under public ownership, as Labour had done in the 1970s only for that measure to be repealed under Thatcher. Second, there would need to be investment in infrastructure including public transport. Measures of this nature could include HS2 (north–south to and from London) and HS3 (east–west between Liverpool and Hull). A third key area would be investment in 'green' technologies such as renewable energies. Finally, investment in human capital improving education and skills.

Two objections are usually made to this kind of reflationary programme.

First, monetarists argued that the Keynesian policy of counter-cyclical fiscal expenditure would be inflationary. A widely held view in the 1960s and 1970s that led both Conservative and Labour governments to impose wages policies was that inflation was seen as being caused by excessive demand in wages from overly-powerful trade unions. In contrast, monetarists argued that inflation was the result of excessive growth in the money supply and was therefore the fault of governments printing too much money. Governments caused inflation, while trade unions caused unemployment. However, investment through government borrowing can only be inflationary if it exceeds the rate of economic growth. Investment such as this would raise economic growth by at least the rate of increased borrowing and probably more as the new investment has wider economic benefits. Hence, it makes economic sense to distinguish public expenditure between investment that will boost growth and can therefore be funded through borrowing, and current expenditure which should not be funded through borrowing.

Second, economic liberals would argue that the state has no role in promoting economic growth. Economic activity is best left to the market and the rate of growth would be higher under free market conditions. One key reason for this is the role of knowledge in driving economic activity. The key influence here is Hayek,[1] who argued that the price mechanism is the result of infinite decisions in the market economy based on 'tacit' knowledge. As this form of knowledge cannot be comprehended by rationalist planners – because it cannot be made explicit and cannot be aggregated – the government will inevitably fail if it intervenes in the economy by disrupting the allocative efficiency of the price mechanism. Along with arguments that planning is always authoritarian in its nature, this is the essence of Hayek's rejection of state intervention. If the government intervenes to 'back winners' it will always fail. Failed experiments in worker cooperatives in the 1970s and the failure of nationalised industries to return surpluses was held up as proof of this assertion. The Hayekian stress on tacit knowledge influenced not only the free-market right but also the so-called 'market socialists' who were influential in the Labour Party from the late 1980s onwards. The role of the state is increasingly defined in neoliberal terms as something that should only intervene in cases of clear market failure and the success of the state sector is measured in terms of the objectives of the private sector. So, for instance, the failure of nationalised industries to make a surplus was deemed to show their failure as they were not subject to competition and the profit motive and should therefore be broken up and sold off.

An anti-austerity agenda must revive the role of the state. There are a range of arguments that can be put forward for a more extensive state. First, state intervention in the economy is necessary to ensure that the private sector is stabilised through effective regulation. This is particularly true of financial regulation, which was clearly lacking in Britain and the United States. Banks had become 'too big to fail' and therefore it was felt that they had to be bailed out. The banks that engaged in routine high street functions – which required stability and careful stewardship of their customers' savings and mortgages – were also involved in the 'casino capitalism' of merchant banking. Reform is still necessary in this area. These two areas of banking need to be separated so that there is more security for retail banking and more regulation of investment banking to avoid the risks that accrued by 2007–08. More local banking may be a desirable policy to pursue. Those economies which were closer to the coordinated market ideal type in Hall and Soskice's model have much greater diversity and plurality of banks than the UK and also have a state-owned bank which would be the vehicle for capital investment. They allow for a greater degree of long-termism compared to the very much short-term emphasis of British banks where long-term investment is discouraged in preference to an immediate return on the capital borrowed.

Second, the only way of securing that externalities produced by private corporations such as pollution are addressed is through a more active state. The neoliberal belief in the supremacy of the market tends to neglect the ability of private corporations to create externalities such as pollution. A recognition of these externalities would fundamentally challenge the exclusivity of the profit motive as the only legitimate concern of corporations. Corporations have duties not only to shareholders but also to employees, customers and the wider community along the lines advocated by Will Hutton in his stakeholder model of capitalism which was briefly advocated by Blair but then dropped in favour of the 'third way' which had a more orthodox view of corporate responsibility.[13]

Moreover, the state has a capacity to recognise forms of knowledge that the private sector cannot. The exclusive focus on tacit knowledge in Hayek's case for neoliberalism ignores the fact that there are other forms of knowledge, particularly in terms of coordination, which only the state can acquire. Mariana Mazzucato argues that the state can fulfil the role of the entrepreneur, in a situation where the risk-averse private sector fails. This can take the form of being the lead risk-taker and the creator and shaper of new product markets.[14] The state alone can do this – in partnership with the private sector – by acquiring coordinated knowledge.

Finally, only the state can rebalance the economy. The British economy is in desperate need of rebalancing both sectorally and regionally. One of the principal reasons why Britain was susceptible to a severe banking crisis and deep recession was the overreliance on financial services after years of deindustrialisation. The economy needs to be rebalanced away from such an overreliance to investment in new forms of productive capital. Although some on the free-market right would regard industrial policy as inherently backward looking, there are high-tech modern industries in which a British government could invest. The British economy also needs to be rebalanced regionally away from the South East to the rest of the UK. The market has clearly failed in both regards and so the only means by which the economy can be rebalanced is through active industrial and regional policies.

Conclusion

This chapter has demonstrated both that austerity is avoidable and that an anti-austerity and pro-growth agenda is not only desirable but also credible. Much more detail can be added to the basic outline of such a strategy provided here. Labour arguably lost the last election because it was trapped between opposing austerity and wanting to gain credibility defined in a certain way by the Conservatives and the right-wing press, ultimately failing to deliver either convincingly. 'Softer austerity' is not a satisfactory position as Labour will always be outdone by the Conservatives on plans to squeeze public expenditure. Equally, moral exhortation against austerity is not convincing either because Labour is thereby reduced to a party of protest. However, as we have seen a strategy which rejects austerity but also has a clear plan for economic growth and a revitalised political economy of the state is clearly feasible.

Notes

[1] W. Hutton, *How Good We Can Be* (London: Little Brown, 2015), p 231.

[2] J. Schumpeter, *History of Economic Analysis* (London: Allen and Unwin, 1954).

[3] F. Fukuyama, *The End of History and the Last Man* (New York: Free Press, 1992).

[4] K. Ohmae, *The Borderless World* (London: HarperCollins, 1994).

[5] A. Gamble, *Politics and Fate* (Cambridge: Polity, 2000).

[6] P.A. Hall and D. Soskice, *Varieties of Capitalism: The Institutional Foundations of Comparative Advantage* (Oxford: Oxford University Press, 2001).

[7] The following are all quoted in P Hain, *Back to the Future of Socialism* (Bristol: Policy Press, 2015), p 68.

[8] Hain, *Back to the Future of Socialism*, pp 279–84.

[9] Hain, *Back to the Future of Socialism*, pp 285–7.

[10] W. Keegan, 'Keynes versus household economics' in R. Hattersley and K. Hickson (eds) *The Socialist Way: Social Democracy in Contemporary Britain* (London: Tauris, 2013).

[11] Hain, *Back to the Future*, pp 262–78.

[12] See, for instance, F.A. Hayek, 'The use of knowledge in society' in F.A. Hayek, *Individualism and Economic Order* (London: Routledge, 1949).

[13] W. Hutton, *The State We're In* (London: Cape, 1995).

[14] M. Mazzucato, *The Entrepreneurial State* (London: Anthem Press, 2013).

TWO

Equality

Robert M. Page

This chapter will look first at the question of why the concept of equality has held a pivotal place in British democratic socialist thought. Attention will then turn to the democratic socialist case for equality in the current era before sketching out the framework of a prospective egalitarian economic and social policy agenda for Labour.

Revisiting democratic socialism and equality

While opinion remains divided as to whether Jeremy Corbyn will be capable of steering Labour to victory in the next General Election,[1] his unexpected success in Labour's leadership contest in the autumn of 2015 has provided the Party with a much needed opportunity to re-consider the case for democratic socialism in the twenty-first century, particularly in relation to the notion of equality – the theme of this chapter.

One of the major criticisms levelled against New Labour during its period in office from 1997 to 2010 was its unwillingness to construct an inspiring egalitarian vision, giving rise to the charge that there was no longer any significant ideological divide between the Party and its main political opponents. Although there is merit in this claim, it has to be remembered that New Labour's commitment to Revisionism was far from unique. In the 1950s and 1960s, for example, Revisionists embraced the notion of equality as a way of demonstrating to the electorate that Labour was committed to creating a fairer society under the 'new' economic and social conditions of the time, rather than being fixated on a doctrinal commitment to public ownership. Although this was always a false dichotomy, the intense debate between Revisionists and so-called fundamentalists during this period highlighted the contested way in which equality was discussed within Labour circles.

The ethical case for equality has always formed a central part of Labour's ideology since the Party was formed in 1900. Party supporters believed that the operation of an exploitative economic system which allowed wealthy, property owning elites to amass vast personal fortunes, while working people were forced to endure arduous and exploitative working conditions as well as the perennial threats of poverty, unemployment, ill health and homelessness was morally unjust. An alternative economic and social doctrine was developed emphasising the need to transform social relations, replace unjust economic and social institutions and redistribute income and wealth.[2] There were, however, significant differences of emphasis between the ethical socialists, such as William Morris and R.H.Tawney, and the Fabian socialists. The principal objective of the former was to create a society where fellowship would thrive and where individuals would be able to lead more fulfilling lives. In contrast, Fabian socialists were more concerned with devising practical solutions that would counter the economic inefficiencies resulting from unregulated market activity.

Over the decades there has been near unanimity within Labour circles about the need to bring about greater *social* or *status* equality. As David Miller explains, this involves 'the idea of a society in which people regard and treat one another as equals, and together form a single community without divisions of social class'.[4] While socialists accept the idea that there are discernible differences between individuals they maintain that no characteristic should be permitted to 'crystallise into an overall social ranking'.[5] Unlike a caste society 'in which inequalities of rank are fixed, pervasive and publicly affirmed', the egalitarian society would be marked by 'mutual understanding and sympathy'.[6]

Liberals and 'progressive' Conservatives have lent their support to the democratic socialist commitment to status equality. This has resulted in cross-party accords on legislative change to tackle discrimination based on age, gender, ethnicity, disability and sexuality. Labour's Equality Act of 2010 reflected the Party's continued determination to counter such discrimination and promote a fairer society by bringing together over 116 separate pieces of legislation into a single Act.

Democratic socialists also maintain that individual life chances should not be a matter of luck.[7] As Stewart White (1997) notes, 'Even when there is formal equality of opportunity, some individuals will have significantly lower life-chances...than others due to differences in skills, handicaps, and holdings of wealth...which are simply a matter of differential "brute luck".'[8] It is deemed unjust that some individuals are able to prosper in life purely because they have had the good fortune to be born into a wealthy family or possess some innate talent which is, by chance, highly valued in the market place. In order to negate the impact of luck, democratic socialists have been keen to ensure that all citizens have access, as of right, to the resources and opportunities needed to pursue their self-directed life course. State provision of essential services such as housing, healthcare and education is seen as crucial if all citizens are to have meaningful life chances given the limitations of both market and voluntary alternatives.

There is less unanimity, though, among democratic socialists in relation to economic or material egalitarianism. George Bernard Shaw was of the opinion that all citizens should receive an equal income as of right without reference to economic criteria such as the market value of an individual's endeavours.[9] The only stipulation that Shaw made was that citizens should be required to make some appropriate social contribution. In more recent times, Shaw's ideas have formed the basis for the introduction of 'unconditional' forms of financial assistance (Basic or Citizens' Income). Shaw's approach has, however, been rejected by other socialists who believe that an income guarantee should, at least in the case of the active working-age population, be linked to a requirement to undertake appropriate paid work or some form of education or training.[10]

There are differences of opinion about the constituent features of an egalitarian, or socially just, distribution of income and wealth. Should a degree of inequality be permissible on the basis of innate talent, effort or personal choice provided that all citizens are first guaranteed 'an equal chance to live a minimally decent, fulfilling life?'[11] While objections have been raised about the legitimacy of material inequities resulting from luck or, 'functionless' economic activity which serves no social purpose,[12] a number of socialists are persuaded that economic inequalities which result from personal effort, proficiency or a willingness to undertake more demanding forms of work are acceptable provided that they can be shown to enhance national prosperity. For example, Le Grand contends that it is difficult to object to inequalities which result from the exercise of individual preferences which are *not* a consequence of impermeable opportunity barriers.[13] Crosland, who believed that income inequalities had become less pronounced and less contentious in the post-1945 era, supported higher rewards for those exercising some exceptional ability provided that their contribution was conducive to the good of the nation.[14] For Crosland, the extent of such inequalities needed to be monitored and constrained to ensure that they did not pose a threat to equality of status. While Crosland considered the 20 to 1 'spread from top to bottom' of post-tax income from work in the mid-1950s to be unacceptably wide,[15] he did not, in contrast to commentators such as Meacher[16] set out his own preferred ratio.

While the post-war Labour governments of Attlee (1945–51), Wilson (1964–70 and 1974–76) and Callaghan (1976–79) remained committed, albeit with varying success, to the pursuit of both social and economic equality, there was a clear ideological retreat from this latter tenet of democratic socialism during New Labour's tenure in office under Blair (1997–2007) and Brown (2007–10). Both these New Labour leaders were convinced that Labour needed to jettison its historic support for greater economic equality in the light of changed economic and social circumstances and the decline of collectivist sentiments among the electorate.

Following New Labour's defeat in the 2010 General Election, there was a concerted effort to shift the Party's narrative on economic equality. Under the leadership of Ed Miliband (2010–15) New Labour's championing of market and entrepreneurial activity was scaled back. By the time of the 2015 General Election, Labour was committed to tackling the growth in economic unfairness within the workplace, though its fear of being perceived by the electorate as a 'welfare' party limited its willingness to embrace egalitarian, non-reciprocal forms of social policy.

Contemporary democratic socialist debates about equality

Let us now turn to contemporary democratic socialist debates regarding inequality. Growing economic inequality has been attracting concerted interest in democratic socialist circles in recent years and, more surprisingly, within international economic organisations such as the International Monetary Fund, the Organisation for Economic Co-operation and Development (OECD), the World Bank and the Global Economic Forum.

Although increasing levels of income and wealth inequalities can be detected in most OECD countries in the recent past, this trend has been particularly noticeable in the UK and the United States. In the United States, for example, the top 10 per cent of earners received 35 per cent share of income compared to a 25 per cent portion for the bottom 50 per cent (2010). The wealth distribution was even more unequal with the top quintile receiving a 70 per cent share compared to a 5 per cent stake for the lowest half of the population.[17] This distributional pattern has become even more marked since the mid-1970s.[18] In the UK in there is a similar, though less extreme, pattern of income and wealth inequalities. Currently those in the top 20 per cent of the income distribution receive around 40 per cent of all income compared to an 8 per cent share for those in the lowest quintile. The wealth share of the highest decile is 45 per cent while the figure for those in the bottom 50 per cent is just 8 per cent.[19] Again, this marks a regressive shift from the situation in the late 1970s.

The dramatic growth in the prosperity of the super-rich has led a number of analysts to focus on the position of those in the top 1 per cent of the income and wealth distribution.[20] In 2010 the top 1 per cent of UK earners (an elite group which is itself highly 'unequal') received 13 per cent of total income compared to a share of around 6 per cent to 9 per cent in the period from the 1950s to the end of the 1970s.[21] This trend is reflected most starkly in the growing pay gap between Chief Executives of large companies and other members of their workforce. In the 1950s the CEO to average employee ratio was around the 25 to 1 mark. By the late 1990s this had risen to about 60 to 1 and by 2012 had reached 170 to one.[22] Moreover, a recent report (2016) found that the pay of the two leading US hedge fund managers (each earning 1.7bn per annum) would have provided employment for 112,000 people at the national minimum wage rate of $15,080 (£10,400).[23] The wealth holdings of the top 1 per cent of the population are even more inequitable. Their 53 per cent share (2010) of 'personal tradable wealth' compares to just 6 per cent for those in the lower 50 per cent of the distribution.[24] In the absence of significant egalitarian policies (see below), it is unlikely that these trends will be reversed. As Hills and Stewart (2016) note, on the basis of their forensic examination of key socioeconomic trends since the financial crisis of 2008, there has been a significant reduction in hourly wage rates for the lowest paid male and female workers and little sign 'that the longer run effects of the crisis and recession narrowed wealth differences or led to a reduction in wealth holdings at the top'.[25]

The difficulties which reformist governments have been experiencing in designing and implementing effective re-distributional policies to rein in income and wealth inequalities in the face of a transformed global economic environment has led to growing interest in the notion of predistribution – a term coined by the American political scientist Jacob Hacker.[26] Recognising the limitations of redistributive strategies, particularly in an era in which additional spending commitments might prove politically contentious, Hacker has argued for the introduction of 'progressive' policies which would improve the position of 'squeezed' middle-income earners and those experiencing poverty. This approach would involve less direct spending, except in opportunity enhancing areas such as pre-school education and childcare, but, rather, greater reliance on regulatory 'nudge' measures which would encourage employers to pay higher wages and improve the conditions of their employees through such means as flexible working. Hacker has also stressed the importance of tackling market generated inequalities through tighter regulation of the corporate and financial sectors and through enhanced trade union activity.

In turning to the issue of egalitarian social policy, it is important to note that Labour's longstanding commitment in this sphere was challenged during the New Labour era and beyond. While it proved difficult in the post-1945 era to guarantee that all citizens would have access to a broadly similar range of essential social services such as education, health and social security on the basis of need, rather than on grounds of status, desert, ability to pay or geographical location, earlier democratic socialists did endeavour to even out some of the historic disparities through the introduction of fairer funding and administrative arrangements. Strong central state direction formed a crucial part of this initial process. In the field of social security a universal, nationwide system (albeit on a 'dual' insurance/means-tested basis) was established. In the case of healthcare eligibility for NHS services at either primary (GP) or secondary (following the nationalisation of the prevailing patchwork system of local authority and voluntary hospitals) level was based on a more egalitarian citizenship standard.

Although the New Labour governments of both Blair and Brown remained convinced of the need to retain a strong central government influence in the area of social policy (with Brown effectively functioning as a 'welfare overlord' from 1997 to 2010), no attempt was made to persist with the more radical egalitarian strategies of former Labour administrations. Although New Labour remained committed to the notion of social justice, they responded to global economic and social change and the eighteen-year period of neoliberal Conservative policy by retreating from the Party's long-standing commitment to universalism and state provided services. Under the pragmatic banner of 'what works', New Labour sought to make an accommodation with the tenets of a neoliberal form of public sector management, which involved greater reliance on performance indicators, audit, choice and competition. New Labour also favoured an increased role for private and voluntary sector welfare providers. In terms of equality, the main emphasis was on removing opportunity barriers for the upcoming generation of children and young people through measures such as Surestart, an area-based initiative which aimed to enhance the future welfare of those living in disadvantaged communities. This egalitarian strategy was based on the notion that no child should be held back from reaching their full adult potential by poor schooling, residing in a workless household or being denied access to essential forms of support.

The retreat from equality also formed part of both the 'Blue' and 'Purple' Labour movements that emerged after the Party's election defeat in 2010. Blue Labour thinkers such as Glasman, Rutherford and Stears contend that Labour should abandon its focus on what they believed were unrealisable goals such as equality and social justice and focus instead on relationship building within communities so that more creative, responsive and diverse ways of meeting emerging social needs can be debated and resolved.[27] In an effort to counter what they regard as the impersonal, legalistic and 'inhumane' forms of 'egalitarian' state welfare, Blue Labour recommends a shift from central direction and control to more localised forms of decision making where the allocation of scarce resources such as housing can be made in accordance with community preferences rather than remote, impersonal forms of bureaucratic fiat.

While more cosmopolitan and European in outlook and supportive of globalisation and controlled immigration, Purple Labour (a revisionist New Labour strand of thinking associated with groups such as Progress and Policy Network) shares Blue Labour's concern about equality. They believe not only that that the strength of public support for this principle has eroded,[28] but also that there is growing scepticism about the state's ability to protect citizens from the adverse impact of corporate power. In such a climate, Purple Labour contend that future Labour governments will find it increasingly difficult to generate sufficient tax revenues to meet the escalating cost of the welfare state arising from demographic and technological change. With a limited prospect of significant productivity gains in labour intensive social services, Purple Labour accepts that the Party faces hard choices if it is to meet projected shortfalls in public expenditure. Greater reliance on non-state funded provision is deemed inevitable as is increased diversity and inequity in service provision.

A further challenge to egalitarianism arises from the greater devolution of powers to Scotland, Wales and Northern Ireland as well as to English regions and cities (for example, Greater Manchester and Cornwall).[29] While it can be argued that devolution will allow nations and regions to pursue more egalitarian policies than if they were tied into more unitary national arrangements, there is a danger that the push for localism will lead to a fragmentation of service provision, discriminatory eligibility criteria for services between insiders and outsiders, and corrosive forms of competition between localities for public sector workers such as doctors, teachers and nurses.[30]

The call for more personalised forms of social service delivery to reflect increased diversity also poses a dilemma for egalitarians. While listening to the voice of service users is a vital means of ensuring that services are delivered in ways which best meets the needs of particular groups, it remains the case that the voices of the most articulate and powerful tend to carry the greatest weight in personalisation debates. Greater personalisation is likely to undermine the universalist appeal of Democratic Socialism and give rise to more unequal, individualistic and non-solidaristic forms of service provision.

While democratic socialists have always highlighted the limitations of equalising opportunities rather than outcomes, the difficulties in devising and implementing effective policies which can bring about the latter form of equality have proved hard to overcome. This has led some on the left to focus on changing the current *pattern* of inequality. The focus here is less on tackling the differential reward structures *per se*, but, rather, on ensuring that these unequal rewards are shared more fairly among those deemed 'meretricious' rather than allowing them to be the sole preserve of self-perpetuating elites.[31] For example, the Sutton Trust[32] has been campaigning for educational reforms which will permit 'talented' working-class or disadvantaged children to access the educational resources and opportunities which will catapult them into so-called 'top jobs'. Even with such reform the prospects for increased social mobility remain bleak unless there is a rapid increase in higher-skilled jobs to match those which led to the modest improvement in mobility that occurred in the second half of the twentieth century.[33] It remains doubtful though whether an equivalent expansion of well-paid elite jobs will be achieved in an increasingly globalised era. Without increased job opportunities of this kind the quest for a more 'egalitarian' social mobility will stall unless space is found for aspiring working-class children by means of downward social mobility. Given the substantial efforts which prosperous parents make to ensure that their children remain in elite positions through such means as private education, personal tutors, social networks and internships, the prospects for increased social mobility remain bleak.

Equality: the way forward for Labour

In Labour's General Election manifesto of February 1974 the Party promised to:

(a) bring about a fundamental and irreversible shift in the balance of power and wealth in favour of working people and their families;
(b) eliminate poverty wherever it exists in Britain, and commit ourselves to a substantial increased contribution to fight poverty abroad;
(c) make power in industry generally accountable to the workers and the community at large;
(d) achieve far greater economic equality – in income, wealth and living standards;
(e) increase social equality by giving far greater importance to full employment, housing, education and social benefits;
(f) improve the environment in which our people live and work and spend their leisure.[34]

In devising its contemporary egalitarian economic and social strategy, Labour would do well to reaffirm these 'spirit of '74' commitments. In the process Labour will need to recognise that its contemporary policy agenda must reflect the increased level of global inter-connectedness. It is, for example, now extremely difficult for individual socialist governments to levy effective taxes on multi-national corporations or global elites without significant forms of European and global cooperation in areas such as tax evasion and avoidance and the regulation of tax havens.

In terms of tackling economic inequality, Labour should engage with some of the ideas emanating from influential scholars such as Piketty, Atkinson and Milanovic.[35] The progressive annual *global capital tax* (GCT) proposed by Piketty is worthy of consideration in this regard. Although this measure has a freely conceded utopian feel to it, such a tax could be implemented incrementally thereby helping to create momentum for more radical change. The introduction of GCT would require a high level of global financial transparency such as the sharing of relevant financial data so that an accurate assessment of the assets held by individuals within specific jurisdictions. The new tax would be levied on the market value of all financial assets including bank deposits, shares, bonds and property. Piketty suggests that the annual tax could be varied according to net worth with the less wealthy (200,000 to 1 million Euros) paying a 0.1 per cent rate, while a 1 per cent rate would be imposed on those with wealth holdings of between one and five million Euros. Those with fortunes in excess of this latter figure would attract a levy of 2 per cent.[36] While the income derived from this tax would be relatively modest in the first instance, this should not detract from its cultural significance as a means of promoting global financial transparency and halting exponential increases in wealth inequalities.

Labour should also devise a more egalitarian income tax regime. Atkinson has called for the introduction of both a targeted earned income tax discount (to help modestly paid workers) and a new range of tax bands with an initial 25 per cent rate. A marginal rate of 35 per cent would be levied on incomes above £35,000; 45 per cent for incomes in excess of £55,000 and a top rate of 65 per cent for those whose incomes exceed £200,000. One of the advantages of the 65 per cent band is that it should help to rein in the exponential rise in so-called 'top' pay.[37] It seems clear that the tax cuts afforded to higher income earners in the 1980s led compliant remuneration committees, in both the public and private sectors, to acquiesce with the exaggerated claims of senior executives concerning their 'entitlement' to exceptional rewards. As was noted earlier, there also needs to be far greater debate and transparency concerning organisational wage differentials. There have been calls, for example, to limit 'executive to low paid employee' pay differentials. These range from the modest 75 to 1 ratio currently pertaining between the Chief Executive and those on average salaries in the employee-owned company, John Lewis, to a more egalitarian 6 to 1 formulation in the fair trade organisation, Traidcraft.[38] Labour should also reaffirm the importance of full employment by setting explicit targets in this regard and offer 'guaranteed public employment at the minimum wage to those who seek it'[39] (p 303).

Another way of promoting equality would be to link particular taxes, such as corporation or inheritance tax to specific services such as the NHS. Hypothecation of this kind would serve two inter-related purposes. First, attempts by corporations, or those working in the financial services industries, to avoid making equitable contributions to the Exchequer through tax avoidance or other related measures are likely to experience social opprobrium if their actions are deemed to be having a negative impact on highly valued social services. Second, hypothecation of this kind would help to remind the public of the link between tax revenues and the quality of public services thereby helping to reinforce the socialist case for fairer taxation.

In turning to the question of an egalitarian social strategy Labour needs to throw off the shackles of the New Labour years and adopt a more positive narrative concerning the role and purpose of the welfare state. The welfare state should no longer be portrayed as an outmoded institution requiring 'life-saving' neoliberal remedies such as competition, choice, audit and unaccountable managerialism. Nor should it be regarded simply as a life cycle savings bank.[40] Rather, it needs to be seen as a key component of a transformative egalitarian agenda.

In constructing its new egalitarian social vision Labour should focus initially on the broad direction of travel rather than focusing on 'micro' policies. In the case of social security this would involve setting out the Party's commitment to ensuring that all citizens, particularly those of working age who are only able to work sporadically due to physical or mental ill health, are provided with a regular and reliable form of income. A decision will have to be taken if this goal will best be achieved by an inclusive, reciprocal social insurance scheme, based on some form of 'work' contribution (including non-paid activities of various kinds) or a Basic or Citizen's Income scheme.[41] If Labour opts for the latter it will need to decide whether any conditions should be attached to the receipt of such a benefit and the level at which it would be paid. If it is decided to introduce generous universal awards this would require relatively steep marginal tax rates but with fewer discretionary additions. In contrast, more modest universal payments would need to be bolstered by a number of specific, needs-based additions.

In the sphere of housing, consideration will need to be given to the prospective roles of the owner-occupied and rental sectors before devising the requisite policy instruments to ensure that all citizens, particularly those with additional needs, have access to affordable housing. This will involve a state-led housing drive to meet the growing demand for new, well-constructed homes with good space standards. Labour will also need to set out clear guidelines relating to land ownership, property and land value taxes, the role of social and private sector landlords, rent controls and security of tenure.

In education, Labour will need to return to egalitarian comprehensive ideals promoted by Crosland and others and consider how these can be reshaped for the contemporary age. This will involve exploring the respective roles of central and local government, the long-term future of private, Academy and Free Schools given their socially and educationally divisive impacts and much stronger oversight of colleges and universities, which have become subservient to commercial imperatives.

Labour will also need to ensure that an egalitarian ethos is embedded within the National Health Service and in the area of social care. The development of Foundation Trusts and accompanying competitive and cost-cutting funding processes must be countered if patient care and safety is to be maintained. A complementary egalitarian public health strategy needs to be developed which emphasises the importance of prevention and controls the activities of the commercial sector that undermine the health of the nation. A major reform of social care is also needed. Despite a number of high profile reports[42] highlighting the need for change, there has been little sign of significant action. Social care must be fully integrated within the National Health Service so that a comprehensive, well-funded, state-run domiciliary and residential provision can take shape. This will require a major service reorganisation with significant new investment in staffing and facilities.

Britain remains a deeply divided and unequal society. Labour needs to draw on the substantial body of evidence highlighting the adverse economic and social effects of growing inequality[43] and construct a bold Democratic Socialist egalitarian agenda for the twenty-first century. Labour must ignore those who favour the adoption of defensive, ameliorative 'progressive' political strategies on the grounds that this will help capture 'swing' voters and opt instead for an energising, transformative strategy. This will be a testing task given the high level of popular scepticism concerning politicians, the role of government and the way in which institutional arrangements seem to bolster the vested interests of rich and powerful elites. While Labour will need to be responsive to new ideas and policy proposals in developing its new agenda, its long-term success will only be guaranteed if its policy direction is underpinned by socialist principles rather than unprincipled technocratic fixes. By following this path Labour will be in a much stronger position to persuade the public that they once again have the choice of living in a 'red' and pleasant land.

Notes

[1] See T. Ali, 'Corbyn's Progress', *London Review of Books* 38, 5 (5 March 2016), pp 21–3; R. McKibbin, 'Labour dies again', *London Review of Books* 37, 11 (4 June 2015), pp 11–12; P. Collins, 'The politician who never grew up,' *Prospect*, March 2016, pp 32–6. At the time of writing (July 2016), Corbyn was facing a leadership challenge from Owen Smith after losing the 'confidence' of many Labour MPs.

[2] See B. Jackson, *Equality and the British Left* (Manchester: Manchester University Press, 2007), Part I.

[3] See N. Mackenzie and J. MacKenzie, *The First Fabians* (London: Quarter, 1979); R.J. Harrison, *The Life and Times of Sidney and Beatrice Webb 1858–1905: The Formative Years* (Basingstoke: Palgrave, 1999).

[4] D. Miller, 'What kind of equality should the left pursue?' in J. Franklin (ed.) *Equality* (London: Institute for Public Policy Research, 1997), p 83.

[5] Miller, 'What kind of equality', p 93.

[6] Miller, 'What kind of equality', pp 93–4.

[7] See S. White, 'What do egalitarians want?' in J. Franklin (ed.) *Equality* (London: Institute for Public Policy Research, 1997), p 62. See also K. Lippert-Rasmussen, *Luck Egalitarianism* (London: Bloomsbury, 2015) and R.H. Frank, *Success and Luck* (Princeton, NJ: Princeton University Press, 2016).

[8] White, 'What do egalitarians want?', p 62.

[9] See Jackson, *Equality and the British Left*, pp 60–3.

[10] Jackson, *Equality*, chapter 3.

[11] See White, 'What do egalitarians want', p 69. For a partial defence of economic inequality see, Commission on Social Justice, *Social Justice* (London: Vintage, 1994).

[12] R.H. Tawney, *Equality* (London: Unwin, 1964).

[13] See J. Le Grand, 'Conceptions of social justice' in R. Walker (ed) *Ending Child Poverty* (Bristol: Policy, 1999), pp 65–7.

[14] See C.A.R. Crosland, *The Future of Socialism* (London: Constable, 2006), chapter 7.

[15] Crosland, *The Future of Socialism*, p 164.

[16] See M. Meacher, *Diffusing Power* (London: Pluto, 1992), pp 55–7.

[17] See T. Piketty, *Capital in the Twenty-First Century* (Cambridge, MA: Harvard University Press, 2014), Table 7.2, p 248.

[18] See, for example, L.M. Bartels, *Unequal Democracy* (New York: Russell Sage Foundation, 2005), chapter 1; A. Sayer, *Why We Can't Afford the Rich* (Bristol: Policy, 2015), chapter 1; S. Scheve and D. Stasavage, *Taxing*

the Rich (New York: Russell Sage Foundation/Princeton University Press, 2016).

[19] See Equality Trust data at www.equalitytrust.org.uk.

[20] See, for example, J.S. Hacker and P. Pierson, *Winner-Take-All-Politics* (New York: Simon and Schuster, 2010) and D. Dorling, *Inequality and the 1 per cent* (London: Verso, 2014).

[21] See Sayer, *Why We Can't Afford the Rich*, chapter 1.

[22] See S. Lansley and J. Mack, *Breadline Britain: The Rise of Mass Poverty* (London: Oneworld, 2015).

[23] See R. Neate, 'Top hedge fund managers collect $13bn', *Guardian,* 11 May 2016.

[24] See Dorling, *Inequality and the 1 per cent*, pp 21–2.

[25] See J. Hills and K. Stewart, 'Socioeconomic inequalities' in P. Lupton, T. Burchardt, J. Hills, K. Stewart and P. Vizard (eds) *Social Policy in a Cold Climate* (Bristol: Policy, 2016), pp 245–66.

[26] See J.S. Hacker, *The Institutional Foundations of Middle Class Democracy* (London: Policy Network, 2011) and J. Hacker, B. Jackson, and M. O'Neill, 'Interview: The politics of predistribution', *Renewal*, 21, 2/3 (2013), pp 54–64.

[27] See M. Glasman, 'Labour as a radical tradition', in M. Glasman, J. Rutherford, M. Stears and S. White (eds) *The Labour Tradition and the Politics of Paradox* (The Oxford–London Seminars, 2011), pp 14–34. M. Stears, 'Blue Labour', *Analysis*, BBC Radio 4, 21 March 2011. M Stears, 'The case for a state that supports relationships, not a relational state' in G. Cooke and R. Muir (eds) *The Relational State* (London: IPPR, 2012) pp 36–43. J. Rutherford, 'The future is Conservative' in M. Glasman, J. Rutherford, M. Stears and S. White (eds) *The Labour Tradition and the Politics of Paradox* (The Oxford–London Seminars, 2011); J Rutherford, 'The first New Left, Blue Labour and English Modernity', *Renewal* 21,1 (2013), pp 9–14.

[28] See R. Philpott (ed) *The Purple Book* (London: Biteback, 2011). See also G. Lodge and R. Muir, 'Localism under New Labour', in P. Diamond and M. Kenny (eds) *Reassessing New Labour* (Oxford: Wiley-Blackwell, 2011), pp 96–107.

[29] See H. McKenna and P. Dunn, *Devolution: What it means for Health and Social Care in England* (London: Briefing, King's Fund, 2015); Department for Communities and Local Government and Department for Business, Innovation and Skills, *Cornwall Devolution Deal* (London: Stationary Office, 2015).

[30] See M. Beech and R.M. Page, 'Blue and Purple challenges to the welfare state: How should "statist" social democrats respond?' *Society and Social Policy* 14, 3 (2014), pp 341–56.

[31] For a trenchant critique of the notion of meritocracy see D. Lipsey, 'The meretriciousness of meritocracy', *The Political Quarterly* 85, 1 (January–March 2014), pp 37–42.

[32] See The Sutton Trust website, www.suttontrust.com/.

[33] The issue of social mobility, and its measurement, continues to be the subject of lively debate. See J. Blanden, P. Gregg and S. Machin, *Intergenerational Mobility in Europe and North America* (London: Centre for Economic Performance, 2005); J. Goldthorpe, 'Decades of investment in education have not improved social mobility', *Guardian*, 13 March 2016 and M. Savage, *Social Class in the 21st Century* (London, Pelican, 2015).

[34] *The Labour Party Manifesto 1974: Let Us Work Together. Labour's Way out of the Crisis* (London: Labour Party, 1974).

[35] See Piketty, *Capital in the Twenty-First Century*; AB Atkinson, *Inequality* (Cambridge MA: Harvard University Press, 2015); B. Milanovic, *Global Inequality* (Cambridge MA: Belknap Press, 2016).

[36] Piketty, *Capital in the Twenty-First Century*, chapter 15. See also objections by J. Galbraith, *Inequality* (Oxford: Oxford University Press, 2016).

[37] See Atkinson, *Inequality*, p 152.

[38] See also Hutton's reservations in this regard – W. Hutton, Review *of Fair Pay in the Public Sector: Final Report* (London: Stationary Office, 2011).

[39] Atkinson, *Inequality*, p 303.

[40] See J. Hills, *Good Times, Bad Times: The Welfare Myth of Us and Them* (Bristol: Policy, 2015).

[41] See M. Torry, *101 Reasons for a Citizen's Income* (Bristol: Policy, 2015); H. Reed and S. Lansley, *Universal Basic Income: An Idea Whose Time Has Come?* (London: Compass, 2016).

[42] See Commission on Funding of Care and Support, *Fairer Care Funding: The Report of the Commission on Funding of Care and Support* (The Dilnot Report), (London: Department of Health, 2011); Commission on the Future of Health and Social Care in England, *A New Settlement for Health and Social Care* (The Barker Report), Final Report (London: Kings' Fund, 2014).

[43] See, for example, R. Wilkinson and K. Pickett, (2010) The *Spirit Level* (rev edn), (London: Penguin, 2010); R. Skidelsky and E. Skidelsky (2013) *How Much Is Enough?* (London: Penguin, 2013).

THREE

Welfare

Pete Redford

You would be hard pressed to find a person of left leaning who does not hold the landslide victory of 1945 as the high watermark for democratic socialism in the UK. An era by which all Labour governments who came after will be judged. The establishment of the NHS and the creation of the modern welfare state are held up as the prime example of what democratic socialism can achieve. Whether it is, indeed, fair to base expectations on those achievements is a long and complex debate to which more space is required than allowed here. However, those who do regard this period in such high esteem will always wonder where it all went wrong. Since the end of the post-war settlement and the emergence of neoliberalism the left has struggled to articulate a clear narrative when it comes to the welfare state.

One important lesson that we should always draw from the election of the Attlee government are the possibilities created by a vision and the ability to sell that vision to the country. This is where the job at hand becomes difficult, almost too difficult for those who are inclined to be driven by public opinion and the 'floating voter'. The question is do we fight for the principles that we hold in such high regard or do we 'move with the times'? Of course that is not to say that there is anything wrong with moving with the times, revisionism is key to the survival of democratic socialism, and many of the issues faced today could never have been imagined in 1945. However, we must stop to question the path taken and the development of a strategy that produces 'piecemeal' social policy that attempts to take the rough edges off capitalism, with little success. We must instead discuss the possibility of creating a more far reaching and transformative vision for the welfare state rather than one that provides accommodations to the market, the right and neoliberalism in general.

This chapter seeks to the make the case for a new welfare state fit for the challenges of the twenty-first century. I would like to do this in three parts. First, we must understand the nature of what the welfare state has become. Not just the ideological assault of the Right but also the pervasiveness of neoliberal agency in society. Second, we must restate the case for universalism as the fairest and most practical form of welfare provision. Finally, and what is most important, I would like to propose the transition towards a universal basic income (UBI) based on the principles of fairness and equality. A new welfare state for the twenty-first century in keeping with the democratic socialist vision.

Where it went wrong: conditionality and means-testing

The current UK welfare system began as the Beveridge system of social contribution. A system that was founded on the principles of the need to help the most vulnerable, to provide care and reciprocal altruism; it was the duty of individuals to combine as a society with the strong supporting the weak. The current system has become a shadow of this. By their very nature welfare systems are moral institutions, but the morals these systems represent have evolved with the prevailing moral perspectives of the governing administrations. The entrenchment of neoliberal economic and social policy have shifted the prevailing moral perspective to one which focuses on the behaviour of individuals, that more often than not, focusing on negative assumptions and behaviours. Following the crisis of social democracy in the 1970s these ideals have been eroded by the damaging pervasiveness of neoliberal ideology shifting the moral perspective of welfare institutions to more individualistic, damaging and divisive beliefs.

Dangerous ideas such as Keith Joseph's 'cycles of deprivation' and the idea of households with multiple generations claiming benefits have seeped into the public consciousness despite research providing no evidence to support such claims. The Joseph Rowntree Foundation extensively searched for evidence of intergenerational cultures of worklessness and found no evidence to support the claim.[1] Charles Murray's perceptions of a new British 'underclass' have also had a similar effect driven further in today's media by programmes such as *Skint*, *Benefits Street* and half of Channel 5's schedule. The New Right, in combination with the media, has succeeded in creating a notion of procedural justice and a mental state of 'othering', where the idea of 'strivers vs. skivers', 'fecklessness' and 'scroungers' have become synonymous with the idea of welfare, further leading to a clear distinction being made by the state and in the social conscience between who is 'deserving' and 'undeserving'.

This moral perspective has led to a system of complex incentives, conditions and sanctions. The significant minority in need of support are stigmatised and in many cases victimised for their need of support. The hardening attitudes of New Labour and the muscular approaches of Conservative governments have essentially led to a system facing a legitimacy crisis of declining public support, in turn leading to a series of incremental reforms under the banner of 'conditionality'. Over time this conditionality has meant welfare institutions developing an elaborate set of rules applied in an often capricious manner with many claimants increasingly finding themselves caught in a sanctions trap. In 2014 alone 17 per cent of Jobseeker's Allowance (JSA) claimants were sanctioned.[2] In one particularly shocking case an Employment and Support Allowance (ESA) claimant who had a heart attack during a work capability assessment was sanctioned for not completing the assessment.[3] These sanctions have led to the demoralisation of many who are out of work as well as serious lasting mental health impacts for some. Inevitably they can also lead to growing financial despair with many experiencing poverty, further indebtedness and the growing need for foodbanks, all of these creating a knock-on effect with a further need for help across the public and charitable sectors being created, putting further strain on the system.

A system that requires means-testing and conditionality also leads to a system where many who need help do not receive it. The take-up of means-tested benefits are generally low, only Housing Benefit tops an estimated 85 per cent take-up rate in 2013/14 with the squeeze in the housing market being partly responsible for this. Pension credit only has a take-up rate of between 67–73 per cent and JSA only 59–66 per cent.[4] Means testing by its very existence creates a form of social control with the conditionality and rules of eligibility framed by the prevailing moral attitudes or the ideology of the government charged with administering them. The provision of welfare in 2016 Britain has become unnecessarily complex and harmful both for the individuals who require help and for the way that society sees these individuals.

For a fairer and more sustainable welfare system fit for the twenty-first century means-testing and conditionality need to be a thing of the past. This is why we should look again at a more universal approach to welfare. Universal benefits are more practical by their very nature, as they are given to all regardless of circumstance. They are cheaper to administer and more efficient in their delivery. They can also help to eradicate the poverty trap perpetuated by the means-testing system. A change to a more universal system of welfare creates a system more integrative than a divisive one that has been created by means-testing. Universal systems provide a service based on equality with a clear social vision and a more socially secure society.

The case for universalism

We must regard universalism as key in any democratic socialist vision for the future of the welfare state. It treats all citizens as equals in society and recognises that the needs faced by society are similar to all. The collective need of housing, education and healthcare are best met through collective measures designed so that no individual, and indeed the most vulnerable, should have to bear inordinate costs of unemployment, disability and illness. In order to build a sustainable system two criteria of welfare must be fulfilled. It has to be universal and it has to be non-judgemental. Benefits and services which are only available to the poor or subject to means-testing serve only to further the notion of deserving and undeserving. In both the short and long term these methods of providing welfare have only served to divide and alienate.

A more universal approach to welfare helps to redistribute resources in order to lessen inequalities. The redistributive effects of universalism can provide a catalyst to encourage social integration and encourage fellowship. Richard Titmuss firmly believed in the principles of universalism and unconditional welfare. He wrote, in his final book *The Gift Relationship*, that the defining quality of welfare was its focus upon 'integrative systems: on processes, transactions and institutions which promote an individual's sense of identity, participation and community'.[5] It is evident that Titmuss in his view of universalism was clearly influenced by the more utopian visions in R.H. Tawney's thought on equality. As such he tended to understate human nature and the sinfulness of man. Because of this we must be wary of buying into the idea that universalism automatically creates the society of which Titmuss speaks. Whereas it can play an important role in breaking down socially-constructed divisions such as gender, class and ethnicity in practice it has not always operated effectively.

This is where we must also look at universalism in more pragmatic terms. Arguably, universalism is more likely to take root in more socially homogenous societies and in eras such as the aftermath of the Second World War. Contemporary Britain is more diverse, people are more self-interested, materialistic and a greater emphasis is placed on the differences between us. Therefore it can be argued that people are less inclined to altruism now than ever before. Anthony Crosland argued that there is little importance to creating a 'moral consensus'. Rather, the proceeds of economic growth should be used to redistribute to the poor without antagonising the majority of voters who were not poor. Everyone would be better off but the poor would be getting better off more quickly. Crosland's approach to redistribution and equality clearly makes a more technical rather than the moral case espoused by Tawney and Titmuss. It would be wrong to judge either one as wholly right or wrong but in contemporary Britain I believe it is more practical and pragmatic to make a more technical case for redistribution.

We must also avoid the defensive welfare strategy of the New Labour governments. The unnecessary desire to be the Party of the floating voter led to maintaining and expanding procedural justice in the welfare system. The obsession that welfare policy should mirror public opinion hinders the possibilities of creating a truly transformational and redistributive welfare system. Just because the poorest have less electoral impact does not mean that policies relating to them should be beholden to the opinions of those that do. I am sure that many who are that way inclined of thinking will point to public opinion and research that shows more traditional egalitarian and democratic socialist welfare policies are not popular but this is not what I intend to propose. I believe there is a way of achieving solutions and at the very least significantly alleviating some of the problems faced by the welfare state discussed above. It reflects aspects of traditional socialist thought such as that of Tawney and Crosland and could achieve the support in public opinion that is craved by followers of the Third Way without an unnecessary muscular approach focusing on flaws of the individual.

A universal basic income (UBI)

A much fairer system of welfare is possible and that is why we must make the case for a UBI. A UBI is an income unconditionally provided to all on an individual basis. There is no means-testing or a requirement of employment; a UBI effectively acts as a minimum income guarantee to all citizens. Far from a utopian concept it offers a new form of welfare that can radically alter the British welfare state for the better. As discussed above, our current system has been taken apart under neoliberalism creating a system more focused on conditionally and stigmatisation than the one envisioned by Beveridge and implemented by democratic socialists. This system has failed to tackle unemployment and in many cases perpetuates many societal problems. A UBI provides an opportunity to recapture the vision of the post-war settlement. Paid irrespective of income or status the UBI has the potential to create a new and truly universal welfare state as well as providing the catalyst for redistribution and an end to the unemployment trap created under our current means -tested system.

The idea of a basic income is not a new one, stretching as far back as Thomas Paine and his notion of endowments funded by land rents. The idea has been articulated by academics and philosophers on both the left and right. Prominent among them was Libertarian Socialist G.D.H. Cole. In several books, he resolutely defended what he was the first to call a 'social dividend'. Cole's justification relies on the social basis of current production as a common inheritance: 'Social heritage of inventiveness and skill incorporated in the stage of advancement and education reached in the arts of production; and it has always appeared to me only right that all the citizens should share in the yield of this common heritage.'[6] A UBI offers the opportunity for all to share in the advancements of Britain in the twenty-first century.

The idea of a UBI is receiving unprecedented interest across the globe. Limited trials offering a form of UBI to the unemployed are planned in both the Netherlands and Finland. In June 2016 Switzerland held a referendum on its introduction with 23 per cent voting in favour. While this may seem a crushing defeat the referendum generated significant global interest in the issue. Recent Europe-wide polling has suggested that 58 per cent of Europeans knew about the idea and 64 per cent would vote for a basic income.[7] A growing body of literature has also developed on the subject and the idea is embraced by those on the left and right. It would be quite easy to make a 'utopian' socialist case for UBI but it is important to remain pragmatic in the idea of its introduction. While no scheme of this nature will ever be cost neutral we can introduce a scheme that is practical in 2016 Britain.

There are many different models of UBI that have been suggested and some are a lot more generous than others. Howard Reed and Stewart Lansley's report *Universal Basic Income: An Idea whose Time has Come?*[8] has explored the practicalities of introducing UBI in the UK.

In their preferred model pensioners would receive £51 a week; adults over 25 £71; under 25 £61; children £59. All means-tested and non means-tested benefits would be retained but UBI would be taken into account when calculating benefits, child benefit is replaced by UBI, and the state pension is maintained with UBI paid on top of it. In this we should see the scheme as a transitional approach with the aims of implementing a full UBI scheme in the future eliminating the need for any form of means-testing.

With an annual cost of £209.5 billion this might seem an implausible change to our welfare system. For this scheme to be affordable there would have to be changes to the tax system. UBI income would not be taxed but income tax personal allowance would be abolished. The basic, higher and top rates of income tax would become 25 per cent, 45 per cent and 50 per cent respectively and NIC contributions would be put at 12 per cent on all earnings. When we look at the £209.5 billion figure again and minus the reduction of other benefits replaced by UBI and the increased taxes and NIC contributions the net cost becomes £8.2 billion or 0.5 per cent of GDP. This is easily affordable at a time where a Conservative government can provide £19.5 billion in tax cuts at a time of 'austerity'. The scheme proposed is a practical one based on its implementation under current conditions.

What, however, would we get for this extra expenditure? A truly progressive change of income with some 60 per cent of the poorest fifth gaining 20 per cent more income. The new system would also take a fifth of people out of working tax credits altogether and reduce the number of people dependant on means-tested benefits. A reduction of child poverty by almost a half, working age poverty by a sixth as well as modest reductions in pensioner poverty and overall inequality. For many the cost of £8.2 billion to reduce child poverty by 40 per cent would be worth it on its own but the other benefits also indicate that a UBI is certainly an option we on the left should be taking seriously.

The Royal Society of Arts[9] have also put forward the case for UBI and have raised interesting notions relating to the reinforcement of citizenship with all recipients of a basic income being required to be on the electoral register. This could help promote political engagement among a section of society which needs to be more engaged. There is also a further idea to expect each 18–25 year old to sign a public 'contribution contract' committing to 'earning, learning or caring' this is designed for a positive affirmation to establish norms and create a contribution ethos. Although the practicalities of getting young recipients to commit to the elements described in the contracts are questionable the idea of creating norms of reciprocal altruism are admirable. They have also elaborated on the conditionality of receiving such payments with EU nationals only receiving payments if they have contributed into the system for a number of years as per EU law, international migrants would receive it in accordance with existing rules and those serving custodial sentences would not be eligible.

The case for a UBI

The introduction of a UBI has the potential to alleviate many societal ills and problems with the current system that many of the left will find appealing and in a way that is pragmatic and sustainable. Let us begin with poverty, by providing a guaranteed income floor it can become a powerful tool in tackling the growing problem of poverty both in and out of the workforce. Traditional democratic socialist solutions to this have revolved around guaranteed work and income support. As guaranteed work has become less available and income support has been weakened the left has been wanting of a tool to effectively combat poverty. UBI can help to mitigate the effects of increasingly insecure labour market conditions on the most vulnerable in society.

Another key strength provided by a UBI would be the freedom and choice it can potentially offer. People would have a basic security that can allow for increased bargaining power in the labour market, more choice in the length and type of employment they choose to have allowing for a better work–life balance. A trial of a basic income scheme in Manitoba, Canada found evidence of positive contributions to the health, nutrition, education and mental health of participants as well as fewer overall hospital visits.[10] It can also provide people with more time for childcare as well as greater time given to volunteering and their community. The greater freedom given by the implementation of UBI would particularly be beneficial to women. From a feminist perspective a basic income creates greater freedom for those who provide secondary and unwaged labour. UBI would recognise the contribution of unwaged work such as childcare, housework and caring for family members which are disproportionately undertaken by women. By providing an equal treatment on gender both inside and outside the labour market it can also increase the personal autonomy of women and greater economic independence in the family unit.

There is also a strong economic case for UBI. Although these schemes are inevitably not cost neutral in terms of public expenditure UBI is fair in its distribution; it is also more efficient. It eradicates the need for means testing and cuts down on bureaucracy. It will also reduce or eradicate many of the benefits currently paid in the UK. From a macro-economic perspective it can also be used as an interventionist tool to stimulate the economy at times of stress. Creating demand by topping up the UBI for a period of time is far more preferable to policies such as quantitative easing which results in distribution to the richest and little economic flow to the rest of the economy. Micro-economically the ability of employees to withdraw their labour from low paid and low quality jobs can provide incentives for better conditions or increased pay. It can also allow short-term exit from the labour market in order to retrain and gain further qualifications with a view to improving job prospects and social mobility. More entrepreneurial recipients can also use extra income to explore other opportunities such as setting up small enterprises.

Finally, UBI could also help to 'future-proof' the workforce against technological advancements. In *Economic Possibilities for our Grandchildren* J.M. Keynes predicted a future of widespread technological unemployment, a recent Oxford study has suggested as much as 47 per cent of total US employment is at risk due to computerisation.[11] Srnicek and Williams' recent book *Inventing the Future: Postcapitalism and a World Without Work* sums up the effect of automation of work and the prospects for the workforce as well as the case for UBI very well.[12] Democratic socialism is already facing significant problems electorally because of this issue. With the massive reduction in traditional and 'trade' jobs since the 1970s the idea of the 'traditional voter' is diminishing with it. Many of these 'traditional voters' no longer see the relevance of the left in their day to day lives. In turn many of the Labour politicians representing them have little to nothing in common with them. A new system based on UBI gives the left an opportunity to take back the ground they have lost and be those who stand up for the vulnerable in the eyes of voters again. With many entry level jobs at risk in future from further mechanisation a basic income would provide greater freedom and opportunity to those at risk. It can provide a tool for a fairer distribution of income from new means of productivity rather than the wealth being concentrated at the higher levels of the labour market as has been the case under neoliberalism. For a voter to believe in the idea of democratic socialism again they must buy into the idea of reciprocal altruism and reciprocal relationships beginning with an initial act of generosity, UBI can provide that initial act.

Dealing with problems in making the case for a UBI

Some may question the wisdom of ending conditionality for those who do not contribute or are judged as 'unwilling' to work. To some the idea of UBI would create an even stronger incentive not to work. In essence this is not what the debates around UBI should be about. This argument is a continuation of the stigmatisation prevalent under the current system. By removing means-testing and conditionality, combined with reducing the impact of the poverty trap, proponents of UBI can argue that it can provide an incentive to work. The poverty trap created by means-testing creates a lack of a significant positive differential between no work and low-paid work. By removing the conditionality from the equation you will always have a basic income therefore any work taken will always make you better off. The regular income provided by UBI is not interrupted when accepting a job, UBI can truly make work pay.

The current system based on the Beveridge model and NICs has been gradually eroded away. NICs are no longer a sufficient means of propping up a system which has become too complex. Conditionality and mean-testing have also help to create declining public support and bring an unnecessary stigmatisation to the system. The scheme illustrated above is far from an ideal system but would provide a radical and important shift from the current system. Stigmatisation will always remain but it is hard to criticise someone for receiving a payment you receive yourself. Of course, elements of the current system such as disability and housing related means-tested benefits would have to remain. Dealing with separate issues such as the housing market and the need of housing benefit would require housing policy to bring down costs to enable them to be incorporated into UBI in the long term. This is not ideal but an eventual transition to a full UBI can help to ensure a minimum income floor that can provide a truly universal system.

In the introduction of this new system the left must also ward off the advancement of such a system's proponents on the right. Whereas we could agree on some arguments relating to the freedom of individuals, the arguments of the right are much more sinister in purpose. Advocates on the right support the principles of a UBI system, because to them it can present an opportunity to do away with welfare altogether. They see such a system as providing less state intrusion and providing the possibility of eroding away other forms of social protection. Charles Murray[13] has recently expressed his view of the creation of a similar scheme of a guaranteed income (GI) to replace the welfare state. According to Murray the 'welfare state has become self-destructing, severely degrading the traditions of work and spawning social and economic problems'. Under his preferred programme a $10,000 annual grant would be paid in monthly instalments and would 'eliminate' the need for social security, Medicare and a whole raft of social problems.

In the right's conception of UBI doing away with benefits and replacing the welfare state is at its core and must be warded off completely by the rational and pragmatic case that can be made by the left. UBI should be seen as an advancement of the welfare of all citizens complementing state provision of public services, not a replacement. This is essential in creating a new welfare system where society can enjoy the benefits it can bring. The current system acts in a way which punishes and takes away where possible. It assumes the worst and contributes to a greater sense of othering. Moving away from a system that stigmatises to one shared by all and helping to bring freedom and self-respect to many is a realistic and better alternative to anything provided by neoliberalism or the right.

Some on the left may interpret the true universal nature of UBI as a problem. It may be problematic that it would apply to the rich as well as the poor. However, the scheme proposed is of greater benefit to the poorest in a truly redistributive manner. It also creates a slight reduction in income for the very richest. By its very being a UBI has to be universal, it has to apply to everybody. As seen in the implementation of the Beveridge system universal benefits have a power that means-testing does not. They do not stigmatise, they treat everybody with equal worth. The principle of UBI should be held in the same regard as the NHS, it is for everybody.

Similarly we must also deal with the inevitable questions from the centre left who may not see this approach to welfare as 'popular' enough. Support for a UBI is growing and we must get on board. It provides a fairer and more constructive approach to welfare than anything since the implementation of the Beveridge Report. Taking ownership of the debate and providing a true alternative to the system in place can only build support. A UBI offers the left an approach to welfare that sets it apart and can help offer a path to back to the support among traditional voters lost in their millions during the New Labour years.

A new future for welfare

It is a truly universal system that we should aspire. Universalism and the long-term transition to a UBI system can eradicate the means-tested system which has become humiliating and off-putting for some.

It can help to combat the pervasiveness of the stigmatising dogma of the New Right and in its place provide the foundations for fellowship and a more non-judgemental society. It can help promote individual freedom, particularly for women, and a more socially secure society.

For the left it provides a renewed vision and purpose in relation to welfare with a clear approach to providing fairness and equality in contemporary Britain. The Labour Party has to resist the urge to shy away from welfare as a divisive issue and must once again restate the claim to being the 'party of welfare' and not being ashamed to do so. By providing a clear vision of a UBI system Labour can state a clear purpose and offer a far-reaching solution to the problems of our current welfare system and wider society. Many of the left's greatest achievements such as the NHS and Social Security were initially treated with scepticism but those debates were won. For a Labour Party that is in need of uniting, the UBI offers a bold new idea that suits both sides. That, and the potential to create lasting positive change to the welfare state, makes this debate certainly worth having.

Notes

[1] T. Shildrick, R. MacDonald, A. Furlong, J. Roden and R. Crow, *Are 'Cultures of Worklessness' Passed Down the Generations?* (York: Joseph Rowntree Foundation, 2012).

[2] S. Malik and P. Butler, 'Watchdog asks DWP for "objective and impartial" sanctions statements', *Guardian,* 7 August 2015.

[3] HC Deb, Jobseekers (Back to Work Schemes) Bill, Second Reading, 19 March 2013, Col(s) 839–40.

[4] DWP (Department of Work and Pensions), 'Income-Related Benefits: Estimates of Take-up: Financial Year 2013/14 (experimental)' (London: DWP, 2015).

[5] R.M. Titmuss, *The Gift Relationship* (London: George Allen and Unwin, 1970), p 224.

[6] G.D.H. Cole, *Money: Its Present and Future* (London: Cassell and Co, 1944), p 144.

[7] N. Jaspers, 'What do Europeans think about basic income?', *Dalia Research* (April 2016).

[8] H. Reed and S. Lansley, *Universal Basic Income: An Idea whose Time has Come?* (London: Compass, 2015).

[9] A. Painter and C. Thoung, *Creative Citizen, Creative State: The Principled and Pragmatic Case for a Universal Basic Income* (London: RSA, 2015).

[10] E.L. Forget, 'The town with no poverty: Using health administration data to revisit outcomes of a Canadian guaranteed annual income field experiment' (Manitoba: University of Manitoba, 2011).

[11] C.B. Frey and M.A. Osborne, *The Future of Employment: How Susceptible are Jobs to Computerisation?* (Oxford: University of Oxford, 2013), www.oxfordmartin.ox.ac.uk/downloads/academic/The_Future_of_Employment.pdf.

[12] N. Srnicek and A. Williams, *Inventing the Future: Postcapitalism and a World Without Work* (London: Verso, 2015).

[13] C. Murray, *In our Hands: A Plan to replace the Welfare State* (Washington, DC: AEI Press, 2006).

FOUR

Public services

Simon Griffiths[1]

Strong education, health and welfare systems are crucial to a good society. Yet they have been shaped in recent years by governments sceptical about the ability of the state to provide them. The assumptions underlying recent reforms have often had their roots in neoliberal critiques of state provision. This chapter takes the neoliberal claims seriously, but argues that following those arguments to their logical conclusions leads to more powerful public services, rather than weakening them. Right-of-centre arguments can be used to reach left-of-centre conclusions. The chapter provides an outline of the philosophical justification for an alternative view of public services. As such, it picks out a libertarian strand in socialist and social democratic thought that was often neglected in the twentieth century.[2]

I begin with a schematic overview of some of the key arguments that have shaped the development of public services since the end of the Second World War and examine what social ills those services were trying to mitigate. I then look at the vulnerability of those services to attack as the post-war consensus collapsed in the 1970s. The chapter briefly discusses New Labour's attempt to combine socially-just public services with a relatively free-market economy that would provide the resources necessary to fund them. It concludes with a discussion of the limited and marketised public services of contemporary Conservatism's 'contracting state', and sets out an alternative account of public services designed to give citizens greater autonomy over their own lives.

Public services and the state

The new public services and welfare reforms that emerged from Labour's 1945 election victory were heavily statist. They pulled together a patchwork welfare system, created in large part by the 'new liberal' governments of the Edwardian era. And while it was a Liberal, William Beveridge, who provided an immediate influence for the post-war reforms, their implementation was carried out by socialists, who argued that the state was best qualified to run them. Nowhere was this centralised state control more evident than in the creation of the new National Health Service. As the minister responsible for the foundation of the NHS, Nye Bevan, noted, the system of political accountability and control from the centre was such that a dropped bedpan in his own constituency of Tredegar should resound through the corridors of Westminster. This was control from the centre.

The left's turn to the state after 1945 was in part an understandable response to the vicissitudes of market capitalism. Rather schematically, there have been two broad critiques of markets from the left, which are particularly relevant here. The first critique is quantitative: markets tend to distribute resources, freedom and power in a way that is grossly unfair. This critique is epitomised in Marx's theory of exploitation: the claim that under capitalism the surplus value that is created by the worker's labour is systematically expropriated by the capitalist. The quantitative critique led to an argument for distributive or social justice in most socialist or social democratic thought. Public services play an important role in ameliorating this problem: they theoretically limit inequality in society, directly through welfare payments or indirectly through the provision of goods and services.

A second critique of market capitalism that public services go some way to meeting is qualitative: markets are incompatible with the quality of life which socialists want. Under capitalism, markets produce for profit and not for use; they fail to provide people with what they really need, stifle creativity and foster competitive, rather than cooperative human relations. Critiques of this kind are found in socialist thought from Marx's concept of alienation to R. H. Tawney's comments on 'the sickness of an acquisitive society'. Public services, by contrast, theoretically provided a shelter from the market, where the interaction is not transactional but based on some notion of responsibility, care, or citizenship rights for example. In keeping with this, for much of the post-war period many on the left held that public services should be delivered by professionals – such as doctors and teachers – organised from Whitehall. These workers were seen to be motivated by altruism and contributed to a 'public service ethos' different to that held by those working in the private sector.[3]

Thatcherism, neoliberalism and the public services

The post-war consensus, based on a welfare state planned from the centre, low unemployment, a mixed economy and predictable gradual economic growth, ended in the crises of the 1970s. Keynesianism could no longer keep its promise of economic success. Strikes by public sector workers culminated in the 'winter of discontent' and inflation grew out of control. In 1979, Britain elected a Conservative government headed by Margaret Thatcher, which radically transformed many of those institutions that had provided a foundation for the post-war consensus, including public services and welfare provision.Justifying this transformation were 'neoliberal' intellectual assumptions about the limitations and failings of the state, and a belief in the superiority of the market to provide goods and services.

Broadly speaking, two strands of argument emerged to challenge the post-war settlement. The first claim was about the inefficiency of state planning. When it came to the wider economy, this argument was associated with figures such as Friedrich Hayek, who argued that markets could marry demand and supply in a way that the state could not. In the public sector, the argument about efficiency was phrased in terms of the misalignment of incentives. William Niskanen, for example, argued that public sector workers would follow their own interests, seeking higher pay and better conditions, rather than being motivated by a 'public service ethos' focused upon improving services for users. The result, it was claimed, was a bloated public sector run in the interests of 'producers' rather than 'consumers'. State provision was seen as inefficient.

The second neoliberal argument against the post-war welfare settlement was about freedom. At its most sophisticated this argument draws on a distinction between 'procedural' and 'end state' arguments. The left tend to argue for particular end-states – a 'socially just' distribution of resources based on need, for example. This is theoretically what public services and the welfare state provide. They are justified by the claim that there is a desired 'pattern' or distribution of goods and resources in society. For many on the right, however, there is no convincing way of determining a particular 'end-state' that will have universal agreement. The left tend to argue in terms of social justice, but what criteria should social justice reward? There are many possibilities: effort, merit, need and so on. Many on the left have argued that social justice should be grounded in the idea of 'need'. But why reward 'need' over other criteria? How does one decide the weight of these other values in the theory of social justice? Even making 'need' central to the argument raises various intractable questions. When two needs conflict, what is the higher principle to which one can appeal to resolve the dilemma? What does need consist of? Values are understood here as irreducibly subjective and incommensurable. There is no final value to appeal to in case of clashes, and no way of tidily ranking values in order of importance.

By contrast, neoliberals, of whom Friedrich Hayek was arguably the most significant, argued that markets are procedural: they do not support any particular end-state or 'patterned principle' – they are 'in principle unprincipled'.[4] No philosophically unjustifiable ends are being pursued. We are presented with a procedural system for following our own good in our own way. The only way to achieve the sort of end-states that those on the left desired would be through using the power of the state to subjugate competing value systems, and impose its own version of 'social justice': for example, by distributing welfare or services to one group at the expense of another. Socialism, it was held, ends in the suppression of liberty.

These philosophical arguments for the market were boiled down into simple phrases that informed the political philosophy of Thatcherism: the state was inefficient and the market ensured freedom. These ideas found their practical application in a range of policies that transformed and limited the role the state during the 1980s. This was most obvious in the privatisation of huge swathes of industry nationalised after the Second World War. The public services were also affected. There were attempts to bring down public spending. Claiming welfare became considerably more difficult. Public services were reshaped along market or quasi-market lines. Local government opened its services to provision by the private sector through compulsory competitive tendering. The purchaser–provider split in the National Health Service mimicked the market. Parental choice was, theoretically, introduced in schools, with money following pupils and league tables provided to inform parents, in choices that paralleled the purchase of any other service. By the 1990s public services were extensively reconfigured from the post-war foundations.

Whatever social democrats thought of these arguments, by the 1980s they had a public resonance to which the left had to respond. In the wake of the Labour's catastrophic 1983 general election defeat, the Fabian Society called together a group of sympathetic academics to discuss what had 'gone wrong'. This Socialist Philosophy Group met on a regular basis to begin 'rethinking and reconstructing socialist ideas'. Many of the papers presented engaged, for the first time since the socialist calculation debates of the 1920s and 1930s, with the idea of the market. These papers were then brought together in a 1989 collection, edited by Julian Le Grand and Saul Estrin, called *Market Socialism*, which remains influential today.[5] The arguments advanced by the group in *Market Socialism* and elsewhere took the pro-market case seriously. The chapters ranged broadly across the left, from the proto-Blairism of Julian Le Grand to David Miller's more radical claim that it was 'quite possible to be for markets and against capitalism'.[6] Yet across the spectrum of opinion three important points were made. First, there was a widespread acceptance of the inefficiencies of the state. Second, there was recognition that the right's efforts to argue against the state on the grounds of freedom had gained public purchase and, by contrast, contemporary socialism did not provide a sufficient account of liberty. Finally, there was agreement that, although the pro-market arguments put forward by the right had to be taken seriously, they did not necessitate the kind of policies that the Thatcher government was pursuing.

The arguments of the Socialist Philosophy Group were influential in the modernisation of the Labour Party in the 1980s. The political philosopher Raymond Plant, for example, worked closely with Labour's Deputy Leader, Roy Hattersley, in the run-up to the publication of his book, *Choose Freedom* in 1988[7], while Julian Le Grand later became a Senior Policy Advisor to Tony Blair. Yet some of the subtlety of the group's views on markets was lost during the New Labour years.

New Labour: ends and means of public services

From 1992 to 2007, the British economy grew at a gradual and steady rate, while unemployment remained low. By the time the Conservatives left office in 1997, after four tumultuous terms, the market-based economic growth model that they bequeathed to Labour in their final years appeared successful. As in the post-war period, an accommodation with the market seemed to have been reached – although in a rather different place. This new pro-market settlement allowed Labour to push through the minimum wage, tax the proceeds of a growing financial sector and to spend the money on public services and various forms of welfare support and subsidy. New Labour set out to combine, as Tony Blair claimed, 'fairness with economic efficiency'. It was this accommodation with the market that enabled investment in welfare, health and education.

For some figures associated with New Labour, the attempt to combine the market with investment in public services was a contemporary form of revisionist social democracy.[8] Their case was often made as a twist on Tony Crosland's distinction between ends (or values) and means. (Older versions of the argument date back at least as far as the German Marxist revisionist, Eduard Bernstein, in the 1890s.) Crosland famously claimed that in calling for a greater role for the state in the running of the economy, the Labour left confused ends and means. He argued, contrary to Fabian socialists such as Sidney and Beatrice Webb, that socialism was not about morality and nationalisation ('abstinence and a good filing-system' as he memorably put it) but about certain ends. Crosland quoted Tawney approvingly, 'Treat sanctified formulae with judicious irreverence and...start by deciding what precisely is the end in view.'9 Crosland was in part attacking the obsession with nationalisation among his socialist comrades, when they should have been thinking about how to achieve a more equal society. Under New Labour, Crosland's distinction between ends and means was applied to the public services. Whether the market, state, or the third sector provided a public service mattered less than the successful outcome of that provision. For example, while New Labour introduced private 'Independent Sector Treatment Centres' that provided healthcare to NHS patients, treatment remained free at the point of use. Social justice through good quality public services was still the end or aim of Labour policy, but the means was more likely to be the market than the state.

The critical arguments against markets introduced at the start of this chapter are helpful in examining the limitations of New Labour's approach. First, it was often argued by New Labour's opponents that heavy reliance on market mechanisms undermined the quality of services in favour of a narrow market-based view of efficiency. Public sector providers in health and social care, in particular, criticised the way in which the public service ethos was undermined by the marketisation of their sectors. An approach that views a patient with complex needs as a problem customer, for example, is unlikely to provide her with better healthcare. Similarly, neglecting the public service ethos that drove many workers to the public services in the first place, and treating them as a changeable means to a particular outcome, arguably undermines expertise inherent in public service institutions. This reflects the qualitative critique of markets set out above.

Second, New Labour was complacent that the market could provide constant economic growth – that 'boom and bust' was over – and that this was a secure means of providing long-term investment in public services. As Michael Jacobs has written, 'Over the past five years…the primary problem facing Western societies has not been a consequence of the failure of the state, but of the failure of markets.'[10] The recession that began in 2008 revealed the extent to which the UK economy had become unbalanced, and the vulnerability of an economic strategy that is reliant on the vagaries of global markets to secure its ends. New Labour's failure to articulate clear values, which social democratic policies helped to attain, meant that once the economic storm broke, their reforms were left deeply vulnerable to erosion. The institutions had not been put in place to weather the coming economic storm. Like the post-war social democrats, New Labour was reliant on constant economic growth, which it would share fairly, but it had no clear response once that growth faltered.[11] This is a version of the quantitative argument against markets introduced above.

Finally, while New Labour was relaxed about the means it pursued, it was sometimes less clear in setting out its ends. Increased public spending improved public services, but for what purpose? In line with the pro-market argument, noted above, that the pursuit of traditional socialist goals, such as greater equality, suppressed freedom and was electorally unpopular, New Labour failed to articulate a persuasive reason why increased public spending was a good thing. I return to the point about the 'ends' that the left should be pursuing in the final sections of this chapter.

The contemporary Conservative Party and 'the contracting state'

Since the electoral demise of New Labour in 2010, Conservative Party policy on public services could be interpreted as an argument for a 'contracting state': a state that is 'smaller' and does less directly. In debates that largely repeated those on Thatcherism a generation before, interpretations of Cameron's Conservatism were divided between those who saw it as a 'pragmatic' response to challenging economic times from a centre ground politician and those who interpreted it as an ideological, or even dogmatic, project. I argue that it is the latter view that is most compelling.[12] Contemporary Conservatism involves a belief in what could be termed 'the contracting state', the intellectual underpinnings of which can be traced back through the Thatcher governments to various neoliberal thinkers. This has profound implications for the public services. At the time of writing, the new Prime Minister, Theresa May, has not suggested any alternative to this position. May arguably has a similar 'modernising' Conservative outlook to her predecessor.

The first sense in which contemporary Conservatism involves a 'contracting state' is the reduction of the size of state spending as a proportion of the total economy. This has a direct impact on the investment available for public services. Cameron and those around him consistently put forward an economic position that criticises the 'overspending' of New Labour and focused on the perceived need for economic austerity. In speeches, Cameron depicted state spending as part of the problem, not part of vital investment in public services. The state, for Cameron, was corpulent, out-dated and inefficient. To some degree this strategy was a response to economic crisis, which gave the Conservative leadership a chance to shift their economic policy substantially to the right. Cameron, for example, quickly dropped his 2007 pledge to stick to Labour's spending plans in the wake of the 2007/08 economic crash, in favour of a commitment to rein in government spending. After Cameron's election in 2010 as head of the Coalition government, his Chancellor, George Osborne, introduced an emergency budget, described by experts as heralding 'the longest, deepest and most sustained period of cuts in public services spending' since the Second World War.[13] Since then there has been a sustained, and partially successful, attempt to reduce public spending as a proportion of gross domestic product. This economic model has a direct consequence on the money available for spending on public services. In this sense, contemporary Conservatism is literally about a contracting state.

A second sense in which contemporary Conservatism reflects 'a contracting state', comes from the form that public services increasingly take: the role of the state is largely limited to 'contracting out' services, rather than providing them directly. Since the 1980s there has been a rapid decline in the idea that the state should provide services directly, and a commensurate acceleration of the use of 'contracting' services to external organisations, overwhelmingly in the private sector, wherever possible. This was reflected in the subtitle of the controversial 2010 white paper, *Equity and Excellence: Liberating the NHS* that heralded major reforms to the National Health Service. It was unclear in the paper what the NHS was being 'liberated' from, but presumably it was the inefficiency and lack of freedoms that was seen to be a part of traditional state-run services. The move towards a contracting state was at its most explicit in the 2011 White Paper on *Open Public Services*, which put the argument for opening up state services to 'any willing provider'. The state was now a contractor of services not a direct provider.

These reforms clearly grow in part from the same ideological seeds as many of the changes introduced during the Thatcher period. To some extent these were continued during the New Labour years, although here they were combined with significant investment in health, education and welfare. Contemporary policy on public services is dominated by the assumptions of the contracting state.

Freedom as an end of welfare and public services

How should the contemporary left respond to the contracting state? I argue that there needs to be a clearer focus on the left on the ends that public services promote. In the dying days of Thatcherism, David Miller noted that, 'freedom as a value has recently returned to prominence on the left'.[14] Today we should take seriously the argument that freedom, rather than any particular end-state, must be the central value of social democracy. This takes the neoliberal argument seriously, but it does not accept its conclusions. Other values, such as equality or community, are important, but only in so far as they contribute to the extension of our liberty. The idea that freedom is the goal of socialism was a historically common view on the left – it was a strand running though the work of socialists from William Morris to the new left. Freedom does not demand the imposition of a simple end-state pattern of distribution of which neoliberals would disapprove.

Making freedom the central value of social democracy does not mean, however, accepting the partial account of liberty that neoliberals offered, and which shapes current debates on the public services. The neoliberal view that freedom is nothing more than the 'absence of intentional coercion' – so we are free, for example, if no one is purposefully stopping us from doing something. This partial account says nothing about why freedom is valuable to us. Freedom is valuable because it is a necessary condition of autonomy or self-direction. To have direction over our own lives we need certain goods, resources and opportunities and the ability to use them. This in turn requires education, healthcare, security, a certain level of income and the protection of the law. Thus public services become a way of *enabling* autonomy and freedom. Modern social democracy must be about empowering citizens so that they can make their own choices about the lives they want to lead, and to be as far as possible 'authors of their own lives'.[15] Freedom without this autonomy is worthless.

The call to focus on values sounds rather removed from day-to-day electoral politics – too vague to gain purchase in contemporary political debate. Yet this is what Thatcher managed in the 1980s, claiming an individualistic and entrepreneurial interpretation of freedom and a critique of state inefficiency for Conservatism and constructing a governing narrative around this language. By contrast, New Labour was often reticent about its ends, fearing perhaps that the centre ground did not share social democratic goals. By making the argument in terms of freedom and autonomy, arguments for social democracy can be expressed in terms of 'empowerment' and 'aspiration'. Social democrats need to paint a picture of the good life that they are seeking to achieve. Blair talked about 'choice', but 'choice' is only important if we have the power to use it. By contrast, a rhetoric of 'empowerment for all' is grounded in serious academic debate about freedom, ability and the good life. Today, Labour must make the case that decent public services allow us to be, in important ways, authors of our own lives.

Public services, equality and other values

Can other values that socialists have traditionally cared about, such as community or equality, survive the neoliberal critique set out above and fit into this argument for strong public services? One radical response to the right's argument that no one can impose a distribution of goods (for example, equality of outcome) or a set of values (for example, community or social justice) on anyone else without infringing their freedom is a move to greater 'starting gate' equality or 'genuine' equal opportunity. If it is not possible to come up with a set of criteria by which we can distribute resources, as the neoliberals have argued, then why should some individuals enter the market as adults with far more resources than others? There should be a presumption in favour of equality, rather than the acceptance of the outcome of an historic power grab for resources. 'Starting gate' equality has strong social democratic policy implications for children and young people, of the kind Tony Crosland recommended in his socialist revisionist writings in the 1950s. It justifies substantial investment in youth services, education and help for families. This approach is also highly sceptical about publically funded institutions that create unfair advantage though the provision of 'positional goods' (that is, those goods whose value is at least in part derived from their limited availability, so that they cannot be more widely distributed without altering their value – some private schools would fit into this category, for example) unless these institutions can clearly demonstrate how they contribute to the goal of spreading freedom more widely in society as a whole.

If social democracy is about promoting freedom and autonomy, other traditional socialist values are not ends in themselves, but staging posts on the way to this final destination. The value that the left places on community or fellowship is a good example of this. Working together with others can give us power to do things we could not otherwise have done alone. Such power increases the capacity for agency – or the autonomy – of those working together. This view recognises that individuals are part of a wider society, and that liberties can be extended by looking at how individuals gain power to achieve their goals as part of unions, movements, organisations and communities.

The policy consequences of an approach that recognises the extent to which citizens, through working together, can gain power to achieve their goals, include support for various approaches that help citizens in their communal endeavours. One idea that seems particularly relevant in the public services is 'collective co-production'. This approach involves groups of citizens in shaping and administering services. As such, it means fostering 'horizontal' relationships between citizens in addition to their 'vertical' relationship with the state. Examples of collective coproduction include peer support groups of individuals engaged in particular activities, time banks to coordinate mutual voluntary work, and participatory budgeting at community level. Through working together in various ways, individuals gain greater power to achieve their goals.

The means to good public services

If the goal of social democracy is the extension of freedom, what can we say about the general means that social democrats have at their disposal to achieve that goal, especially when it comes to the provision of public services? The 'contracting state' limits the scope and remit of state provision. New Labour tended to favour the market as the means of providing better public provision, but coupled that with significant investment. Twentieth century social democracy generally relied on the state, believing that politicians and civil servants in Westminster and Whitehall are uniquely able to pull the levers that create a more socially democratic society. Instead, I argue that a focus on the wider 'ecology' in which public services operate would allow us to get beyond the market/state dichotomy.

In the public services, a variety of approaches must be taken to create more socially democratic ends. The metaphor of 'an ecology' is sometimes used to describe the relationship between the state, market and other providers.[16] Ecologies need careful management, protection and long-term care. Under this view, the state provides support for certain activities to flourish (for example, civil society groups that offer specialist services that meet the complex needs of users or private sector organisations offering innovative approaches to a problem) while managing those areas where the ecology is less healthy (where the private sector dominates all else or public service providers are failing). The state manages the ecology, of which the market, social and public sectors are interrelated parts. The state is sometimes involved directly, but often it facilitates, supports, nurtures or governs other organisations.

In public policy terms, this approach allows greater collaboration between and within public, business and social sectors in order to achieve its ends. This approach is being pushed forward in contemporary public policy by various organisations that explore the conditions and conduct needed for collaboration to be a success between sectors, arguing that each have distinct expertise and capabilities. Under this view it is an empirical question which sectoral 'blend' of providers best meets social democrats' objectives around the extension of freedom.

Recognising the distinct expertise and capability of those who provide public services is also important. Although the argument advocated here implies a relatively relaxed approach to how public services are provided as long as they promote freedom, it would be very cautious about undermining traditional means of public service provision and the public service ethos. That ethos in itself is responsible for one of the most successful means of securing the high-quality public services we have. While drawing on the private and third sector can inject innovation and efficiency to public services, this does not mean an approach that accepts 'whatever works' despite its wider consequences.

This argument about freedom and the public services suggests two main roles for national government. First, it promotes the overall strategic direction of policy towards the extension of freedom and autonomy. This is a head-on response to neoliberalism. Second, in the public services, the state governs an ecology, ensuring that it is balanced and sustainable over the long term. This takes planning and care, but provides a variety of means to extend freedom. It is an empirical question about which blend of providers best serves that goal. In addition, those at the centre must recognise their limits. There are many times that individuals are granted more power to achieve their goals through forms of government above or below Whitehall and Westminster. This approach accepts the limits of the traditional nation-state approach to social democracy. For example, it is only through international cooperation that global markets can be regulated and taxed; and through local government and community involvement, individual freedom can be extended.

Conclusions

For the left, public services largely developed as a way of protecting people from the inequalities and self-interest of market capitalism. For much of the twentieth century, Labour saw the state as the best means of achieving the ends that public services provide. These arguments came under sustained attack as the post-war consensus collapsed. Under the Thatcher governments of the 1980s and the 'contracting state' of today, policies were pushed forward that owed their philosophical justification to neoliberalism. This chapter takes the libertarian goals of these arguments seriously. However, it argues that a logical consequence of following them through is not contemporary Conservatism's contracting state, where spending on public services is constantly squeezed and the state's role is increasingly limited to contracting services out to the private sector. Instead, the consequence of placing freedom at the core of the argument is a discussion about what services and resources one needs to live a free life. This means a decent education system, good healthcare and a strong welfare system. Libertarian assumptions, followed through, lead to left of centre conclusions. Labour must fight for the idea that public services are not just a safety net, grudgingly hung out for those in need, but a way that all citizens can gain more autonomy over their own lives.

Notes

[1] This chapter has a very long genesis. Rather different versions were given to the first meeting of the Social Democratic Philosophy Group at the House of Lords in July 2010, the Institute of Public Policy Research in November 2010 and as a response to Policy Network's 'A Centre-Left Project for New Times' published by the organisation online (http://www.policy-network.net/pno_detail.aspx?ID=4221&title=The-ends-and-means-of-social-democracy-) in July 2012. Later, Matt Beech, Beth Foley, Dan Greenwood, Paul Gunn, Kevin Hickson and Jeff Masters gave helpful comments. Errors and omission remain my own.

[2] In this chapter 'social democracy' and 'socialism' are used almost interchangeably. While the two terms have rather different implications in contemporary British politics (in large part because of the split between Labour and the new Social Democratic Party in 1981) they have historically tended to cover overlapping ideologies, which occupied large areas of the same ground.

[3] For a relatively recent discussion of these issues see P. John and M. Johnson, 'Is there still a public service ethos?' in A. Park, J. Curtice and K. Thomson, *British Social Attitudes* (London: Sage, 2008).

[4] F. Hirsch, *The Social Limits to Growth* (London: Routledge and Kegan Paul, 1977), p 119.

[5] S. Estin and J. LeGrand (eds) *Market Socialism* (Oxford: Clarendon, 1989).

[6] D. Miller, 'Why markets?' in S. Estin and J. LeGrand, *Market Socialism*, p 25.

[7] R. Hattersley, *Choose Freedom* (London: Michael Joseph, 1987).

[8] An argument for the revisionist roots of New Labour is made in P. Diamond, *New Labour's Old Roots* (Exeter: Imprint Academic, 2004).

[9] Quoted in C.A.R. Crosland, *The Future of Socialism* (London: Jonathan Cape, 1956), p 97.

[10] M. Jacobs, 'Beyond the social market: rethinking capitalism and public policy', *The Political Quarterly* 84, 1 (2013), p 16.

[11] An argument developed in A. Painter, *Left Without a Future? Social Justice in Anxious Times* (London: IB Tauris, 2013).

[12] I examine 'Cameronism', draw parallels with earlier debates on 'Thatcherism', and set out an interpretation of the 'contracting state' elsewhere. See Simon Griffiths, 'Cameron's contracting state' (forthcoming).

[13] R. Chote, *Post Budget Presentations: Opening Remarks* (London: Institute of Fiscal Studies, 2010), www.ifs.org.uk/budgets/budgetjune2010/chote.pdf.

[14] D. Miller, 'Why markets?', in S. Estin and J. LeGrand, *Market Socialism*, p 32.

[15] The exact bundle of resources required for autonomy is a matter of considerable debate. It is the subject of much of R. Plant, P. Taylor-Gooby and H. Lesser, *Political Philosophy and Social Welfare: Essays on the Normative Basis of Welfare Provision* (London: Routledge, 1980) and elsewhere. The overall argument in this section around freedom and social democracy owes much to Raymond Plant's work, summarised in a series of Fabian pamphlets published during the 1980s and 1990s and more recently in *The Neoliberal State* (Oxford: Oxford University Press, 2010).

[16] I. Marsh, 'The Blair governments, public sector reform and state strategic capacity', *The Political Quarterly* 80, 1 (2009), pp 33–41. Many of the issues raised in this chapter were also discussed in S. Griffiths and H. Kippin, 'Introduction' in S. Griffiths, H. Kippin and G. Stoker (eds) *Public Services: A New Reform Agenda* (London: Bloomsbury Academic, 2013).

FIVE

Social cohesion

Jasper Miles

Social cohesion is a broad topic, yet one of fundamental importance for the Labour Party to confront. While other factors such as economic credibility and political leadership are important issues to address in order to win the 2020 general election, the Labour Party is required to ease the concerns of a number of British voters and convince them that the Labour Party is 'on their side'. 'Mistrust about our instincts and values on identity and culture-related issues' wrote Ivan Lewis MP in 2011, 'is one of the key reasons why voters have rejected social democratic parties across Europe. In an age of austerity that suspicion will remain unless we are willing to break free from outdated comfort zones.'[1] Defeat in 2015 highlights that mistrust continues to exist. It is the opinion of the author that two major issues will pose considerable challenges to the Labour Party over the course of this Parliament; immigration and the rise of Englishness.

Anecdotally, a recurring theme on the doorstep in 2015 was the message that 'Labour doesn't stand for people like me anymore.' Instead, the Labour Party allegedly stood for foreigners, migrants and welfare claimants. Statistically, the opinion polls highlight that immigration has become increasingly salient over the past decade, and it is clear that voters regard this matter as a high priority. The issue is not a simple left–right split, in which you can easily fit voters into one of two camps.

The Labour Party contains a cultural split predominantly based on social class, in which the middle-class social liberals – generally at the top of the Party – emphasise the economic and pluralistic benefits of immigration whereas working-class Labour voters tend to be more socially conservative, concerned about the pace of change in *their* community, and the impact on British and arguably more specifically English culture and identity.

The rise of Englishness and an English political culture poses an equally significant problem for the Labour Party. Traditionally class-based issues were synthesised with Britishness, with grievances redressed across Great Britain through reforms enacted at Westminster. However, post-devolution and with the rise of Scottish and, to a much lesser extent, Welsh nationalism there has been a growing realisation that Britishness – a bond built upon Empire, military, the Protestant faith, industry and trade union membership, binding all the home nations together has weakened, thus bringing into question the future of the United Kingdom. The decline of voters identifying as solely British and instead solely English or English and British raises both cultural and constitutional questions for the Labour Party. The competing nationalisms in Northern Ireland are of no less significance, yet, because the Labour Party competes electorally only in Great Britain and a different party system exists in the province, along with a general cross-party agreement at Westminster on dealing with the Irish question, this chapter will assess the changing nature of identity focusing only on mainland Britain, specifically the 'English question'.

Many of the issues raised by immigration and the rise of Englishness challenge traditional assumptions about identity, culture and values. Moreover, they are intertwined and go to the heart of issues that should concern social democrats: community, belonging, nationhood and the lives and lived experience of working people in Britain. Therefore, the purpose of this chapter is to outline why both issues have taken on increasing importance with the electorate, how they pose significant political and policy problems for the British left and add to the growing debate on how social democrats should respond in order to create a broad electoral coalition. Focusing firmly on the attitude of the electorate is key, as Maurice Glasman, the Labour Peer behind *Blue Labour* correctly stated: 'We've got to listen and be with them. They're in the right place — it's us who's not.'[2]

Immigration

'Controlling immigration is both consistent with Labour values and a duty of all responsible governments.' (Ivan Lewis MP[3])

The Labour Party has a long and proud history of fighting for racial and social equality and such a proud record should be celebrated and continued. However, while the moral purpose of the Labour Party is a more equal society regardless of colour, ethnicity and background, it must not prevent an examination of immigration. The past two decades, in which 13 years were under a Labour government, witnessed unprecedented levels of immigration into Britain, changing communities many of which had previously seen very little immigration. For example, Boston in Lincolnshire changed from overwhelmingly white British to having the highest proportion of east European residents in any town in Britain and many British cities are now recognised as 'super-diverse' global cities. Added into this mix is a European-wide migration crisis with migrants seeking to enter Britain from North Africa and the Middle East, the threat of Islamic terrorism on British streets and the changing British economy through globalisation and deindustrialisation.

Sections of the British left continue to be influenced by the anti-racism movements of the 1960s and 1970s, subscribing to the cultural benefits of immigration based on a metropolitan cultural liberalism and internationalism, promoting a pluralistic and diverse society. Consequently, they remain wary of criticising mass immigration for being tainted with connotations of racism, xenophobia and a fear of upsetting immigrant communities. Additionally, the overall economic benefits of immigration are professed, especially for big business; filling jobs where there has been a shortage of skills in the labour market and keeping costs down for both the producer and consumer. Indeed, the argument that public services, including the National Health Service, benefit from immigration is often utilised, with doctors and nurses employed from all over the world.[4]

Reducing the argument to a simple economic cost–benefit analysis, however, or considering that once economic disparities are eradicated – low pay, poor quality jobs, lack of housing – or that concerns over immigration is solely the result of globalisation and deindustrialisation is to miss the wider concerns about community, identity and nationhood. Although less tangible than economic factors, the belief that communities are no longer 'ours' should be foremost in the minds of social democrats who value fraternity, common bonds and rooting individuals into communities where belonging and meaning is provided. Given that it has generally been working-class communities that have experienced the fastest rate of change – 'the housing estates of Sheffield not the lovely homes of Hampstead'[5] – there is both the moral imperative and a crude political necessity to respond to the concerns and consequences of mass immigration. The attitude and lived experience of working-class people should not be dismissed or discounted, for the Labour Party was formed to represent such people. Indeed, it is these voters who will help to deliver Labour MPs in both safe and marginal constituencies, and provide the bedrock for a future Labour government. Should the Labour Party fail to address the concerns of socially conservative voters, these voters will punish the Labour Party electorally by looking for political alternatives

The cultural disconnect between the Labour Party and sections of its electoral base became increasingly evident during the New Labour era, exacerbated through high profile incidences involving Labour politicians, and policy decisions by the last Labour government. Pat Glass MP, while campaigning for a Remain vote in the EU referendum in May 2016 in the marginal constituency of Erewash, labelled the first voter she met as a 'horrible racist' for their views on a Polish family, who were supposedly claiming benefits, promising not to return to the area, 'wherever this was'. The electoral strategist for Ed Miliband, Lucy Powell MP, commissioned a document advocating moving the conversation on to more comfortable ground should immigration be raised on the doorstep. Emily Thornberry MP when on a visit to Rochester and Strood during a parliamentary by-election in 2014 took a picture of a working-class home draped in the flag of St George, tagging the photo with the line 'image from Rochester'. Gordon Brown during the 2010 general election campaign labelled Gillian Duffy, a Labour voter concerned with immigration and its impact on jobs, as a 'bigot', although would later apologise.

While New Labour had a commitment to 'protect borders', over the course of 13 years, certain policy decisions on immigration have since helped form the narrative that the Labour Party was weak on border control. Moreover, the Party was on the side of immigrants rather than British people; the liberalisation of work permits, a large increase in foreign students, making it easier to bring spouses into the UK through scrapping the 'primary purpose rule' and increased difficulty in deporting criminals due to the Human Rights Act. Most notably the opening up of the British labour market to the new EU states of Eastern and Central Europe in 2004, seven years before most other countries, led to a large influx of eastern European migrants. Modelling carried out by the government suggested that numbers would be in the region of 20,000. Tristram Hunt MP has since written:

We simply have to acknowledge that the post-2004 immigration influx is the biggest demographic surge in the history of England, creating the fastest growing population we have ever seen… between 2005 and 2007 whilst over half a million incomers found employment more than quarter of a million British workers lost theirs. Of course there is no direct link between the jobs gained and lost…Nevertheless, this legacy has left a toxic political cocktail: communities – our communities – have seen their way of life change, and believe that their economic fortunes have suffered because of a Labour policy for which democratic consent was never sought – let alone given. Even worse we sometimes (seemed) determined to delegitimise complaints and concerns about it.[6]

Indeed, it was claimed that mass immigration had a 'driving political purpose'. Andrew Neather the former adviser to Tony Blair, Jack Straw and David Blunkett, claimed it was to 'rub the right's nose in immigration and render their arguments out of date'. Relaxation of controls was intended to 'open up the UK to mass migration' but ministers were nervous and reluctant to discuss such a move publicly for fear it would alienate its 'core working-class vote...In part realising the conservatism of their core voters' not 'necessarily a debate they wanted to have in working men's clubs in Sheffield or Sunderland'.[7] Yet the 'conspiracy' theory offered by Neather is rejected. Far from intentionally having a plan to change the demographics of Britain, the Labour government had no plan at all, candidly admitted by Ed Owen, a special advisor to Labour's former Home Secretary Jack Straw, resulting in 'policymaking by crisis'.[8] Consequently, the electorate will be expecting a future Labour government to enter office with a clear, thought-through and importantly robust policy on immigration, thus fostering trust and accountability with the British people. A number of suggestions are outlined below based on social democratic principles.

Immigration will remain a key issue for the foreseeable future, especially now that the United Kingdom has voted to leave the EU, and voters will duly be expecting a tightening of controls on immigration to result from the Brexit negotiations. The task of shaping the post-Brexit debate on immigration for the Labour Party is difficult, due to a resurgent Conservative Party who have a headline immigration policy of reducing net immigration down to the tens of thousands. Whether the numerical target is politically wise or indeed a target in the tens of thousands attainable, the principle is correct, and any future Labour government would do well to follow suit. There is also the electoral threat posed by the United Kingdom Independence Party (UKIP) in Labour's industrial heartlands, predominantly in northern England but also in parts of Wales. The populist appeal of UKIP has managed to win the support of many former Labour voters, playing on the legitimate concerns of the older, white, traditionally Labour working-class voters – the 'left behind' – who have experienced rapid social change, through deindustrialisation and changing communities.

Frank Field MP stated in the 2010 general election that UKIP had only managed to recruit 138,000 voters who previously had voted Labour. In 2015 nearly a million Labour voters supported UKIP candidates. Almost a quarter of UKIP's vote in 2015 came from voters who in the 2005 general election had voted Labour.[9]

Yet, the task facing the Labour Party is not insurmountable, and it should seek to build on the leadership of Ed Miliband who attempted to move the Labour Party on from New Labour's negative association with immigration. This was an attempt to regain credibility, and align the Labour Party with socially conservative voters, in the knowledge that this was vital in order to win. Miliband understood 'Eastern European immigration is a class issue because it increases competition for jobs, particularly those at lower wages. It looks very different if you are an employee rather than an employer. But we refused to recognise that sufficiently.'[10] Redgrave observed Miliband's twofold approach: first, immigration was talked about much more, past mistakes were acknowledged along with people's legitimate concerns, and a mainstream position adopted around the notion of managed migration. Second, policies were rooted in social democratic values, including stronger regulation of labour markets to avoid exploitation and the undercutting of wages and conditions of British workers, more border agency staff patrolling British borders, clamping down on people who trafficked and exploited migrants, preventing serious criminals entering Britain and forcing immigrants to learn the English language.[11]

As stated, an explicit commitment to significantly reduce net immigration into Britain should be made, especially unskilled and low-skilled workers, thus addressing both political and cultural necessities. Uncontrolled and unlimited immigration means that British workers can be undercut by cheap foreign labour, and research suggests that for those at the bottom of society, there is a negative impact on their wages.[12] Public services also face challenges including in health, education and housing where increased usage places pressure on a finite resource. The British workforce should be up-skilled making the British economy less reliant on migrants, with a particular emphasis on adult education. Evidence suggests that immigration reduces the willingness of non-immigrants to finance welfare benefits out of taxation and therefore has the potential to build up resentment and undermine a more generous social democratic welfare system. Sergi Pardos and Jordi Munos investigated welfare and immigration, looking at which type of benefit is most undermined by immigration, discovering that targeted benefits are more vulnerable than universal benefits.[13] Given that Britain is experiencing austerity, and is likely to do so for the foreseeable future, continuing high levels of immigration makes the option of targeted benefits by a future Labour government less politically acceptable.

Moreover, the pace of change in communities has, as previously mentioned, significantly altered the demographic makeup of British towns and cities, raising issues of community cohesion and integration. Managed immigration would allow the Labour Party to pursue a positive integrationist agenda, actively encouraging immigrants to adopt 'the British way of life', through practical measures such as speaking the English language and understanding British history, institutions and culture. Integrating migrants would offer greater opportunities for those coming to Britain to engage in civic activities and greater economic benefits, increasing life chances as a good standard of English will increase employability. Indeed, the architects of multiculturalism from the 1960s and 1970s were dismayed by its unintended consequences, with Lord Lester QC admitting on a *BBC2* documentary:

> The model we had was that everyone would share the broad values of being British. What we did not expect was there would be those who unwisely suggest that, for example, Sharia Law should be applied in this country, or that the punishment of stoning for adultery might be looked at depending on the kind of stoning...It never occurred to us that there would be those kind of unwise challenges to the broad values of a liberal democratic society. And I remember towards the end of Roy Jenkins' life him saying to me that we just didn't realise that in the

struggle for race equality that we would also have to struggle for a secular society and for the universal value of human rights.[14]

In light of international and domestic factors social democrats should move away from multiculturalism and metropolitanism and pursue a policy of integration, supported by an explicit commitment to significantly reduce net immigration. While correcting economic injustices is important, concerns about immigration are rooted in identity, community and belonging, and it is on these factors that the Labour Party should focus its attention. The narrative of the Labour Party 'not being for people like me' will persist if the Labour Party does not regain the electorate's trust, pouring doubt on the future electoral success of the Party. A positive integrationist stance, actively encouraging immigrants to adopt 'the British way of life', asserting common values and rules, many of which are social democratic principles, through practical measures and applied in no uncertain terms, will lead to stronger and more united communities. 'Belonging' is found in strong communities, whether that be work, family, community networks, sports clubs or faith groups and under broad 'British values' respect for diversity can flourish.

'Englishness' and the constitutional future of the United Kingdom

In 1941 George Orwell wrote that England was 'the only great country whose intellectuals are ashamed of their own nationality. In Left-wing circles it is always felt there is something slightly disgraceful in being an Englishman and that it is a duty to snigger at every English institution, from horse racing to suet puddings.[15]

At one time it was common for England and Englishness to be used interchangeably for Great Britain and Britishness. However, recent political and social developments have caused a shift, in which the terms England and Englishness have lost their British connotations. Indeed, the flag of choice of spectators at England sporting events was the Union flag and there was no debate about the appropriation by

England of the British national anthem 'God Save the Queen'. The rise of an English political culture and identity poses serious questions for the British left, namely social, cultural, identity and constitutional. As the opening quotation from Orwell suggests, sections of the British left have not always acknowledged the value and importance of national identity.

Dismissing the importance of nationalism as reactionary, backward and invariably right wing is the height of political unwisdom, for voters across the class spectrum and across Britain value nationhood. Indeed, dismissing patriotism is to underappreciate the underlying patriotic current in British socialism that has found expression in a number of institutions and events: defeating fascism on the continent, a belief in internationalism and exercising British influence through international organisations, an independent nuclear deterrent and a strong military presence and, domestically, a welfare state created to deliver social justice across the country based upon need, financed out of general taxation, embodied in the National Health Service (NHS). A generous welfare system and nationalised industries can be a way of uniting people across Britain. 'Those who challenge Labour's patriotism' wrote Lewis, 'should be reminded that the pursuit of a fairer, more united, country where every citizen is given the chance to pursue their potential is patriotism in action'.[16]

While patriotism would have originally been around the British nation, the weakening bonds of 'Britishness' and the decline in those identifying as British, instead identifying as English, presents the Labour Party with a political dilemma. Traditionally, the strength of the Labour Party's faith in the Westminster Model and the British nation, led Ken Morgan, the leading Labour historian and biographer to write that the former Labour Prime Minister James Callaghan viewed 'as most Englishmen did, moves towards devolution as concession to parochial nationalism, in conflict with the central power of Cabinet and Parliament, as well as with socialist notions of planning'.[17] Indeed, the Labour Party relied on Scottish and Welsh MPs to deliver parliamentary majorities, becoming the dominant parties in these parts of Britain and it was thought that the growth in nationalist demands in the 1960s and 1970s on the Celtic fringe would decline once the economic situation improved.

Eighteen years in opposition, however, led the Labour Party to reassess the United Kingdom's constitutional arrangement. New Labour's constitutional reform agenda left a constitutional imbalance in which Scottish MPs could continue to vote on English matters but not *vice versa* – the West Lothian question. In addition, through the Barnett Formula, England was not only subsidising other parts of the Union but arguably doing so to the detriment of England. While the warnings about the consequences of devolution had long been predicted – 'the end of Britain' and a 'motorway without exits to independence' – the future of England as five-sixths of the Union would be key to the future of Britain and the British nation. Yet, New Labour's constitutional reform agenda had little to say about England. *The Dog That Finally Barked* noted that the English identity was becoming politicised, with the more strongly English a person feels the more likely they are to believe that the current structure of the post-devolution UK is unfair and there should be an English dimension to the governance of England.[18]

In a recent survey conducted by the British Electoral Studies and Ian Warren, a quarter of voters identified primarily as English and nearly half as English and British whereas only a fifth were British or more British than English. Moreover, those who identified as English only were much more likely to support UKIP or the Conservatives, while those who were only British were inclined towards Labour. Labour members identified more strongly with Britishness than Englishness. John Denham, the former Labour MP believes this does matter electorally, as Labour cannot afford to ignore those with a strong sense of English identity as their votes helps to deliver Labour MPs and Labour majorities.[19] The fracturing of the political system and the rise of English, Scottish and Welsh nationalism across Great Britain means that the Labour Party is increasingly fighting different electoral battles: the Conservatives in England, Plaid Cymru in Wales and the SNP in Scotland. In addition, there is also the threat of UKIP in a number of Labour constituencies. The idea that there is a distinct 'English interest' not identical with a 'British interest' became more apparent in 2015, and with the Conservative's and UKIP's greater ability to 'speak to England', the Labour Party is in danger of allowing its opponents to shape the debate, away from a social democratic vision of patriotism.

Englishness as a distinct political community is unlikely to revert back into a 'British interest', and therefore will continue to pose the question of whether the Labour Party should commit to political recognition for England and the form, if any, this should take. Peter Hain has argued for regional devolution within a federal United Kingdom with the nations – and potentially the English regions as well as London – federating upwards, granting to the central UK state only those powers and responsibilities they wish, turning the UK into a voluntary federal union of England, Scotland, Wales and Northern Ireland.[20] However, New Labour's attempts to introduce regional parliaments were rejected and dropped after the North-East voted against the proposal in a referendum, and the prospect of an extra layer of democracy is unnecessary and excessive, on top of the layers of democracy currently in existence. Federalism suffers from a number of drawbacks: England would continue to dominate the UK in a number of measurements, it would not sedate Scottish nationalist demands for independence, Stormont would be expected to deliver on a vast range of policy having shown little ability to deliver on minimal policy areas and the constitutional upheaval brings into question whether a scheme would be workable.

Although identifying as English might be on the increase, defining Englishness is more complicated. Regional, economic and social disparities are difficult to bridge, with the South-East of England (London and the surrounding areas) which is far more prosperous than the rest of England, and is far more densely populated. Economically, this area dominates the English economy due to the financial services, whereas the decline in industry and manufacturing in the Midlands and the North is to some degree still being felt, as historically, these areas were more industrialised. The economy of the South-West is based largely on agriculture and tourism, with a much lower population density. Culturally, as Hickson writes, most people do not think in terms of regionalism, but have an affinity to their immediate home area and often their county but not their region. Therefore, it is problematic to fit these economic and cultural variations into a single English identity.[21] Consequently, an English Parliament does not fit easily into an English identity. Moreover, numerically, English MPs are overwhelmingly dominant at Westminster, and a consequence of devolution has meant that legislation emanating from the British Parliament predominantly applies to England.

The Conservative government's response has been English Votes for English Laws (EVEL) dismissing the constitutional expert Vernon Bogdanor's assertion that, 'it is in fact not possible to separate English matters from Scottish'. The Royal Commission on the Constitution in 1973 concluded that: 'Any issue in Westminster involving expenditure of public money is of concern to all parts of the United Kingdom since it may directly affect the level of taxation and indirectly influence the level of a region's own expenditure.'[22] EVEL also causes a practical problem for a Labour government, namely, that unless it can win a parliamentary majority through winning England, it is likely to be reliant on Scottish and Welsh MPs. While EVEL is, as Bogdanor's critique suggests, imperfect it is, according to the polling evidence, popular and *Taking England Seriously: The New English Politics* found this to be the preferred option ahead of an English Parliament.[23]

The Labour Party should commit to this English dimension in policy making for it is Westminster that largely determines what happens to English public services. However, any further parliamentary reforms that lead to the exclusion of Scottish, Welsh and Northern Irish MPs from the decision-making process should be treated with caution, for they could lead to renewed demands for independence. The problems outlined with federalism and English parliament means that the Labour Party's constitutional policy towards England must in part be influenced by the success or otherwise of the Conservative government's 'northern powerhouse' and city regions strategy. Should the devolving of fiscal matters among other policies, to areas such as Greater Manchester, prove to be successful then a Labour government should seek to pursue and enhance the policy. By devolving power internally in England, a form of political recognition is offered, although not to England as a political entity.

The Labour Party should seek to maintain and promote the Union and the integrity of the British State. Gordon Brown, during the 2014 Scottish independence referendum, epitomised Labour's unionist and social democratic values, emphasising the historical, cultural, social and economic benefits of the Union between England and Scotland. Brown had previously written with Douglas Alexander that through the sharing of risk and pooling of resources that has reinforced British citizenship so that all contribute towards 'social protection against sickness, incapacity and widowhood and towards the pensions of each other' and a common purpose avoids 'liberty (descending) into a selfish individualism or into a crude libertarianism'.[24] In spite of the current difficulties of the Scottish Labour Party, the British Labour Party should seek to build upon the patriotic strand in social democratic thought, remaining staunchly unionist, defeating the nationalists through argument, not by pandering and attempting to be better nationalists than the SNP.

Of greater importance than the constitutional question is the way in which the Labour Party can foster and nurture a genuine and authentic civic English patriotism. Given that England is a land of authors, poets, artists, culture, sporting triumph, history, natural beauty and an ingrained sense of 'fair play', many key facets are already in existence, for an open and confident Englishness. With the increased presence of the flag of St George, a commitment to a St George Bank Holiday would be one option to tap into English sentiment. Another could be to have an English Labour Party to respond to the English political community, similar to the Scottish or Welsh Labour Party, under the umbrella of a British Labour Party, who would maintain control over the economy, defence and foreign affairs.

While the Labour Party has to once again become an electoral force across Great Britain if it is to form a government it must recognise and understand the rise of Englishness and respond to those who wish to express their sense of nationhood. The electoral decline of the Labour Party in Scotland means that the Labour Party in England requires a 13-point lead over the Conservatives to make up for losses in Scotland. By 'speaking to England' the electoral gains required are more likely to emerge. Although Scottish politics have changed significantly, a revival in Scotland would be aided to a certain degree by emphasising to voters north of the border that the Labour Party can win in England. The Labour Party could then convince Scottish voters to return to the Labour fold, who they will then deem as the best protection against the Conservatives. In addition, it would help quell voter's fears that the Labour Party would do a post-election deal with the SNP – a tactic deployed successfully by the Conservatives in 2015 – as the Labour Party would be able to promote and defend the 'English interest'.

Conclusion

The ability of the Labour Party to develop a clear, credible and deliverable policy on immigration and Englishness will be vital, if the Labour Party is to win the 2020 general election. People across all social classes and areas of the country have a deep and sincere attachment to the strong bonds of national identity – British and specifically English – and to their local community. The unfortunate tendency of some on the British left to resort to condescension, dismissiveness and labelling those who take a different view as racist or xenophobic reduces the potency of these words when deservedly employed and importantly for the Labour Party, appears to be contemptuous of sections of the electorate, many of whom are traditional Labour voters. A sceptical working-class electoral base should be of primary concern to the Labour Party who value *their* nation and *their* community. Consequently, a pledge to reduce immigration is important not just economically, but also culturally and socially.

Should the Labour Party continue to be at odds with the attitude of voters, then winning a parliamentary majority becomes increasingly difficult. The Labour Party should tap into its social democratic patriotic tradition because seeking to increase opportunity and life chances for all citizens is patriotism in action. Being perceived as anti-patriotic and disrespectful of culture, community and identity is a damning indictment of any political party seeking to govern the British State. There is no compromise with the electorate and the views of the electorate will not change unless the Labour Party can show that it has listened, understood and has clear, coherent and credible policies to address their concerns, thus ending the perception that the Labour Party is out of touch with working people's day-to-day concerns. In doing so it will emphasise to a sceptical electorate that the Labour Party will not shirk the difficult decisions when in office and will 'speak for England'.

While the solutions offered in this chapter are by no means an exhaustive list they offer practical reforms allowing the Labour Party to tackle head on immigration and the rise of Englishness. Failure to grasp both issues will allow Labour's political opponents to take the initiative and, more worryingly, allow both issues to become the preserve of fringe political parties.

Notes

[1] I. Lewis, 'One nation Labour: Tackling the politics of culture and identity' in R. Philpot (ed.) *The Purple Book: A Progressive Future for Labour* (London: Biteback, 2011), p 231.

[2] 'The Fabian interview: Maurice Glasman', *Fabian Review*, Summer 2011, p 8.

[3] I. Lewis, 'One nation Labour', p 242.

[4] The Rt Hon Harriet Harman MP, Remain Campaign Speech, The Oval, Kennington, 6 June 2016.

[5] P. Collier, 'Immigration's "dark side": A challenge for the left', *Policy Network*, 5 December 2014.

[6] T. Hunt, 'Introduction', in T. Hunt (ed.) *Labour's Identity Crisis* (Winchester: Centre for English Identity and Politics, The University of Winchester, 2016), p 7.

[7] Neather's claims originally appeared in the London *Evening Standard*. Quoted in the *Daily Telegraph*, 'Labour wanted mass immigration to make UK more multicultural, says former adviser', 23 October 2009.

[8] See E. Owen, 'Reactive, defensive and weak' in T. Finch and D. Goodhart (eds) *Immigration under Labour* (London: IPPR, 2010), pp 15–16.

[9] F. Field, 'Patriotism and the Left', in K. Hickson and J. Miles, *The Labour case for Brexit* (London: Labour Leave, 2016), p 41.

[10] E. Miliband, *The Labour leadership: How important is it that the Party has a distinctive ideology?* (London: Fabian Society, 2010), pp 55–66.

[11] H. Redgrave, 'Migration: A Social Democratic response' in A. Harrop and E. Wallis (eds) *Future Left: Can the Left respond to a changing society?* (London: Fabian Society, 2016), pp 41–2.

[12] 'Limits on Migration: Limits on Tier 1 and Tier 2 for 2011/12 and Supporting Policies', Migration Advisory Committee, November 2010, Para. 7.88; 'The economic impact of immigration', *Vol 1 Report, House of Lords Select Committee on Economic Affairs,* 1st Report of Session 2007–08 (HL Paper 82–1) para 78; 'International migration and rural communities', Department for Communities and Local Government, March 2011, 3.2.1; 'The impact of immigration on occupational wages: evidence from Britain', *Staff Working Paper* 574, The Bank of England, December 2015; C. Dustmann, T. Frattini and I. Preston, 'The effect of immigration along the distribution of wages', *Discussion Paper* 03/08 (London: Centre for Research and Analysis of Migration, Department of Economics, University College London, 2008).

[13] Quoted in Collier, 'Immigration's "dark side"'.

[14] 'Rivers of blood', BBC2, Saturday 8 March 2008.

[15] G. Orwell, *The Lion and the Unicorn: Socialism and the English Genius* (London: Searchlight, 1941).

[16] Lewis, 'One nation Labour', p 240.

[17] K.O. Morgan, *Callaghan: A Life* (Oxford: Oxford University Press, 1997), p 361.

[18] R.W. Jones, G. Logde, A. Henderson and D. Wincott, *The Dog That Finally Barked, England as an Emerging Political Community* (London: Institute for Public Policy Research, 2012).

[19] http://labourlist.org/2016/04/john-denham-labour-cannot-win-in-england-unless-it-understands-england/.

[20] www.fabians.org.uk/england-in-a-federal-uk/.

[21] K. Hickson, 'The social and economic context', in B. Jones and P. Norton (eds) *Politics UK* (London: Routledge, 2014, 8th edn), pp 41–2.

[22] Quoted in the *Guardian*, 'Why English votes for English laws is a kneejerk reaction', 24 September 2014.

[23] Meanwhile, support divided between EVEL and an English parliament in *The Dog That Finally Barked* found support crystallising around EVEL, www.ipsos-mori.com/researchpublications/researcharchive/3610/Most-support-English-votes-for-English-laws-with-Conservatives-most-enthusiastic.aspx.

[24] G. Brown and D. Alexander, *Stronger Together, The 21st Century Case for Scotland and Britain* (London: Fabian Society, 2007), pp 8–9.

SIX

Civil liberties

Judi Atkins

Civil liberties have been a longstanding concern for the Labour Party. In the words of its 1945 general election manifesto: 'The Labour Party stands for freedom – for freedom of worship, freedom of speech, freedom of the Press. The Labour Party will see to it that we keep and enlarge these freedoms, and that we enjoy again the personal civil liberties we have, of our own free will, sacrificed to win the war.'[1] However, the means used to secure these freedoms have changed significantly since the Party's inception, shifting from a collectivist focus on group rights negotiated by the trade unions or the state to an approach designed to empower citizens as individuals. The first part of this chapter demonstrates that the British socialist belief in civil liberties has traditionally been expressed in universal welfare entitlements and a commitment to protect individuals from arbitrary state action. Both have been challenged in recent times due to the 'war on terror' and an ongoing period of austerity, and the chapter argues that a reaffirmation of these principles is needed in order to promote Labour's longstanding goals of freedom and social justice. Finally, the chapter argues that Labour should act as a champion of civil liberties. In particular, it should ensure a better balance between liberty and security; strengthen civil liberties while harnessing them to their concomitant duties; and promote social justice through a vigorous defence of our economic and social rights.

Civil liberties and British social democracy

Social democrats have traditionally adopted a collectivist view of civil liberties, seeking to empower people through group rights negotiated by the trades unions or the state. As Roy Hattersley puts it, democratic socialism required the 'use of collective power to increase individual rights and to extend individual freedom'.[2] These rights were not only political but economic and social, and, in the context of the welfare state, were present in universal entitlements to, for instance, housing, education and welfare benefits. By redistributing resources in this way, Labour sought to reduce inequality and so promote freedom and social justice.

For most of the twentieth century, many social democrats rejected constitutional reform as the means of securing individual rights and freedoms. In Stephen Driver and Luke Martell's words, they feared that, 'if Labour fought to give more power to (unelected and conservative) judges, the judges would use these powers against a radical Labour government'. By the late 1980s, however, the Thatcher governments' systematic centralisation of power had undermined our long-cherished civil liberties. In response, a group of social democratic scholars and activists created Charter 88, an organisation that campaigned for constitutional reforms to prevent the development of an 'elective dictatorship' in Britain and protect civil, political and human rights. It also outlined ten specific demands, among which were a Bill of Rights that guaranteed basic civil liberties, proportional representation, and 'freedom of information and open government'.[3]

The launch of Charter 88 coincided with the policy review taking place within the Labour Party. By 1989, this process had generated proposals to replace the House of Lords with an elected second chamber, the primary purpose of which was to uphold human rights legislation. As Driver and Martell explain, this approach was widely viewed as a 'better way of securing individual freedom than a formal bill of rights', though some leading modernisers, such as Roy Hattersley, remained concerned that it would hand too much power to the judiciary.[4] The move towards constitutional change gained momentum under John Smith's leadership and culminated in the wide-ranging reforms enacted in New Labour's first term of office. New Labour's flagship legislation in relation to this discussion was the Human Rights Act (HRA) (1998), which incorporated the European Convention on Human Rights into UK law and represented an important step in strengthening civil liberties. However, the rise of consumerism and the attendant commoditisation of rights ensured that their accompanying duties were neglected. The Brown government recognised this and published a Green Paper outlining a 'Bill of Rights and Responsibilities', though its proposals were never enshrined in law.

The contemporary socialist case for civil liberties

Security and liberty are prerequisites for a healthy democracy. As such, the state has a duty to protect the right to life of its citizens, while also upholding their basic freedoms. This can be easier said than done, as the New Labour governments would discover in the wake of 9/11 and the London bombings of 7 July 2005. Driven by the fear of further attacks occurring on its watch, a concern that was heightened by the emergence of the home-grown suicide bomber, New Labour introduced a raft of draconian anti-terrorism legislation. Indeed, despite the protests of its constituent parties in opposition, the Conservative–Liberal Democrat coalition – and subsequently David Cameron's majority Conservative government – followed the same trajectory when faced with the threat of so-called Islamic State. Although the aim of defending the nation against terrorist attacks is commendable, there is no place for detention without trial, secret courts and the like in an advanced democracy such as Britain. Thus Labour must address the current imbalance between liberty and security, while maintaining a respect for human rights and the rule of law.

Civil liberties have also come under threat from the ongoing austerity programme. In order to save up to £350 million, the Coalition removed legal aid for a range of civil cases, including employment, welfare benefits and housing except in limited circumstances. It is perhaps no coincidence that these changes came into effect at the same time as the Coalition's welfare reforms, notably the Personal Independence Payment for people with disabilities and the notorious 'bedroom tax'. Benefits claimants now have no means of challenging the government's decisions, and justice is rapidly becoming a privilege rather than a right in austerity Britain. This contravenes the principle of access to justice for all, while the Cameron government's welfare reform programme is continuing to push thousands of people into poverty.[5] Given the Conservatives' on-going hostility to the HRA, this assault on civil liberties is not unexpected. Labour should therefore reassert their commitment to social justice, while vigorously resisting Conservative plans to replace the HRA with a British Bill of Rights.

The remainder of the chapter sets out a manifesto on civil liberties for the Labour Party. This programme is structured around three themes: a better balance between liberty and security; a clear framework of rights and responsibilities; and a defence of our economic and social rights. Each theme will now be discussed in turn.

A better balance between liberty and security

First and foremost, Labour needs to end the abuse of state power. In particular, it should introduce a system of proper checks and balances that will provide both proportionality and accountability. Human rights legislation has an important role to play here but, for it to be fully effective, Labour must opt back in to Article 5 of the HRA and so put an end to indefinite detention without trial. It also needs to make the procedures for dealing with terrorism suspects more transparent. Under the draft Investigatory Powers Bill (2015), the Home Secretary is authorised to grant access to personal internet and mobile phone records in 'urgent cases'. Given that, as Alistair MacDonald QC observes, many requests are likely to contain some element of urgency, the proposed legislation places too much power in the hands of the Secretary of State. To rectify this, Labour should accept Liberty's recommendation that suspected terrorists should be dealt with using existing laws. This would help to ensure proportionality while placing counter-terrorism operations firmly within the criminal justice system, where they can be subjected to the proper scrutiny.

As an alternative to control orders and the Terrorism Prevention and Investigation Measures (TPIMs) that succeeded them, Labour might extend the regime of police bail to terror suspects. At present, a person on pre-charge bail may be required to provide notification of residence, surrender their passport, report regularly to a police station and avoid specified places or individuals. The imposition of such conditions would allow terror suspects to be monitored while the police and intelligence agencies undertake further investigations, and so render secret courts redundant. However, there is currently no time limit on these conditions, which means that an individual can remain on bail indefinitely. Given that the courts would view this as an 'abuse of process', Liberty proposes a statutory limit of six months for conditional bail, accompanied by the 'usual express legal duty to investigate expeditiously within that period'. This would help to safeguard civil liberties, while giving the courts an important role to play in overseeing the police bail system.

Instead of the Conservatives' proposed Investigatory Powers Bill, which violates both the right to privacy and the presumption of innocence, Labour could make more use of the Regulation of Investigatory Powers Act of 2000 (RIPA). This legislation gives the authorities the power to access data for specific purposes, such as the prevention of crime or in the interests of national security, and its scope could easily be extended to counter-terrorism. The measures available under RIPA include: direct surveillance (for example, the monitoring and filming of suspects, usually in public places); intrusive surveillance (for example, filming in private places and bugging); the intercepting of communication with a warrant from the Home Secretary; and access to the record (though not the content) of telephone calls, emails and websites visited. Currently, police can ask ISPs and mobile phone companies to surrender a suspect's communications data for a maximum period of 30 days. Liberty suggests that this limit could be extended to six months, with the possibility of renewal by a judge. This, along with the other RIPA powers, would enable the police and security services to gather evidence without alerting potential suspects and facilitate criminal trial. With this aim in mind, Labour could also lift the restriction on the use of evidence obtained through intercepts in terrorism trials, a move that would increase the likelihood of prosecution without endangering civil liberties.[6]

Taken together, these changes would bring counter-terrorism within the criminal justice system, where it can be subject to proper oversight. If this strategy is to be effective, however, Labour must ensure that the police are adequately resourced. Since 2010, the policing budget has been reduced by 14 per cent in England and Wales, which to date has meant a loss of 17,000 frontline jobs. While crime is continuing to fall, preventative policing is beginning to suffer and officers are hampered by out-of-date technology. Labour must invest in both of these areas, along with the training and retention of surveillance officers, if it is to preserve local policing and aid the fight against terrorism. Such an investment would be partially offset by the abolition of TPIMs, which Liberty claims would save millions of pounds every year.[7]

An increase in the police budget must be accompanied by the introduction of more stringent checks and balances. Recent scandals such as the Hillsborough cover-up, the efforts of the Metropolitan Police to smear the family of Stephen Lawrence and the unlawful killing of Ian Tomlinson by an officer at the G20 protests have gravely undermined public confidence in the police, and Labour must take action to restore this trust. To this end, it could give more powers and resources to the Independent Police Complaints Commission, which would enable it to investigate and resolve complaints more quickly, and to impose tough sanctions on officers who are found guilty of misconduct. These measures would strengthen the existing framework of standards and accountability, while promoting a culture of openness within the police force.[8]

Although the nation's security is undoubtedly important, it must not come at the cost of our liberty. It is unacceptable that the measures introduced by successive governments to tackle the terrorist threat have undermined the same democratic values they are supposed to protect, and Labour must take steps to rectify this. After all, counter-terrorism and civil liberties are not mutually exclusive, and the proposals outlined above demonstrate that these two priorities can in fact work together. If this less draconian approach, with all its attendant risks, is the price we must pay for remaining a free society, then so be it. On this basis, Labour needs to remake the case for civil liberties, but in doing so it must ensure that they are paired with their attendant duties. The next section provides a prescription for achieving this.

A clear framework of rights and responsibilities

At a time when the HRA is under threat, Labour must publicly renew its commitment to this legislation and to Britain's relationship with the European Court of Human Rights. It should also take steps to counter the negativity surrounding the Act by providing clearer guidance on its use for the courts and the government alike. This would help to ensure that the HRA is properly applied, and thus improve its public image. However, the HRA places a disproportionate emphasis on individual rights, to the detriment of social responsibilities. To correct this imbalance and further increase support for civil liberties, Labour needs to pair them with their concomitant civil duties. The Brown government's proposals for a Bill of Rights and Responsibilities provide a useful starting point for this, though they require further development.

Although many civil duties are already present in statute and common law, they 'have not been given the same prominence as rights in our constitutional architecture'. To remedy this, a Bill of Rights and Responsibilities should clarify what individuals are entitled to expect from the state and from one other, and supply an ethical framework that gives practical expression to our shared values. In common with the HRA, a Bill of Rights and Responsibilities would not contain a mechanism for legal enforceability, on the ground that 'the imposition of new penalties is unlikely to be the best way to foster a sense of civic responsibility and encourage respect and tolerance for others and participation in the democratic process'. Nevertheless, a new constitutional document would enhance public understanding of our civil duties, and thus strengthen the imperative to perform them.[9]

The Green Paper outlining the Bill of Rights and Responsibilities identifies a number of duties that we all owe as citizens. Among them are: the protection and promotion of the welfare of children in our care; the respectful treatment of NHS staff and other public sector workers; civic participation in the form of voting and jury service; respect for environmental limits; and other, more general, duties such as obedience to the law and the payment of taxes. A greater emphasis on these obligations, together with the recognition that rights must be exercised responsibly, would help to build a society that is fairer and more cohesive. To demonstrate this, the chapter will now consider our civil duties relating to the criminal justice system and to the environment.

As noted above, the HRA guarantees the liberty and security of person unless they have been convicted of a crime and sentenced to a term of imprisonment (Article 5), and also the right to a fair trial (Article 6). Other legislation sets out the rights of victims of crime, which include special support for vulnerable witnesses and government compensation for injuries caused by violent crimes. A Bill of Rights and Responsibilities would bring these different entitlements together in one place, enabling Labour to commit itself anew to the basic liberties that have been so badly abused in the name of national security, and to counter the objection that the HRA prioritises the rights of criminals over those of victims.

While it is clear that we have a basic obligation to obey the law, we also have another – perhaps less obvious – duty to uphold it. In England and Wales, for instance, there is a legal requirement to report serious crimes, notably terrorist activity and money laundering. Moreover, citizens are legally obliged to obey a summons to provide evidence in a criminal trial, to tell the truth while under oath, and to serve on a jury. These duties are vital to the rule of law, and a Bill of Rights and Responsibilities should raise public awareness of their role not only in maintaining the justice system, but also of their relationship to our civil liberties.[10]

A healthy environment is a prerequisite for the enjoyment of all human rights. In the light of climate change and the increasing strain on natural resources, a clear statement of our environmental obligations is urgently needed. To this end, the proposed Bill of Rights and Responsibilities adopted the framework elaborated in the UK's 2005 Sustainable Development Strategy, the goal of which is 'to enable all people throughout the world to satisfy their basic needs and enjoy a better quality of life, without compromising the quality of life of future generations'.[11] At the heart of this strategy lies a belief in collective responsibility, though its practical implications are not elaborated in the Green Paper. The remainder of this section outlines some of our basic obligations relating to the environment.

Recycling is a cornerstone of sustainable development. As such, each individual has a duty to recycle as much as they can, and local authorities should facilitate this through, for instance, kerbside collections and the provision of recycling services for public sector organisations. The government, meanwhile, can play an important role not only in regulating and monitoring waste management, but also in building new recycling plants. Such infrastructure projects are expensive, but they would give the economy a much-needed stimulus and, in the longer term, will reduce the amount of waste that Britain ships overseas for reprocessing. However, there are limits on what can be achieved without the involvement of the private sector, and there is plentiful scope for Labour to address this.

The Bill of Rights and Responsibilities focuses on the duties owed by the state, citizens and the public sector. Consequently, the question of corporate responsibility is neglected. On the environment, for instance, the Bill suggests that a 'form of duty' may be imposed on public sector bodies, whereas big businesses are to be merely 'encouraged' to adopt sustainable practices. There is a serious imbalance here, and Labour needs to mount a strong challenge to these powerful elites. Taking the example of domestic recycling, it is evident that supermarkets and manufacturers have a duty to reduce waste, as well as to use recyclable packaging wherever possible and ensure that it is clearly labelled as such. If they fail to fulfil these obligations voluntarily, government should compel them to do so through legislation. The same principle can be extended to other areas covered by the Bill of Rights and Responsibilities, such as tax. After all, if individuals have a duty to pay their taxes in full, then multinational corporations should not be exempt from their obligation to do the same. To date, the Conservatives have refused to tackle corporate irresponsibility, and it is up to Labour to take action in the interests of creating a more just society.

For social democrats, civil liberties and civil duties are two sides of the same coin. Every individual has the right to exercise their freedom, but in doing so they must be mindful of the responsibilities they owe to other people and to society as a whole. These obligations underpin the notions of collectivism and cooperative action, so a stronger link between civil liberties and civil duties will foster a sense of common citizenship. This in turn could act as a powerful corrective to the individualism that has characterised the post–1979 period, and thus begin to heal the wounds caused by the shameless 'divide and rule' tactics that have featured heavily in political discourse since 2010.

A defence of our economic and social rights

In addition to ensuring a better balance between civil liberties and their associated duties, Labour should promote and defend our social and economic rights. More specifically, it could make the case for the full incorporation of the European Social Charter (ESC) into UK law. So far, this move has been resisted, with opponents arguing that it would shift the responsibility for resource allocation from the government to the courts. However, as with the HRA, the courts could be given the power to interpret legislation in the light of the Charter and to issue declarations of incompatibility if required, though not to strike down laws that conflict with its principles.[12] This would help to increase government accountability, while giving more protection to those who need it.

Among the entitlements set out in the ESC are the right to protection of health (Article 11), the right of the family to social, legal and economic protection (Article 16), and the right to housing (Article 31). These rights are fulfilled primarily by the public sector and the welfare state, which have borne the brunt of austerity. As a result, the social safety net is being dismantled and state support is rapidly becoming accessible only to those in the greatest need. Given that thousands of people are only one pay packet away from homelessness and that inequality is widening steadily, the consequences of these policies will be disastrous for many. A wholehearted commitment to the ESC would enable Labour to begin building a fairer, more equal society, in which the most vulnerable citizens receive the protection they so badly need.

The Conservative-led welfare reform agenda has brought misery and hardship to many families and individuals. Since April 2013, the under-occupancy penalty, or 'bedroom tax', has come into force, and benefits have been capped at £26,000 per family per year, though this is set to be reduced further. Moreover, the rates of tax credits and working-age benefits have been frozen for four years from April 2016. These changes, in conjunction with the continued failure of wages to keep up with inflation, have led to an increase in the number of children living in poverty and a sharp rise in food bank use across the UK. That thousands of people, many of whom are in work, cannot afford to feed themselves and their families in the world's seventh richest nation is nothing short of scandalous. It is also contrary to Articles 30 and 16 of the ESC which, respectively, enshrine the right to protection against poverty and social exclusion and guarantee an 'adequate standard of living for families'.

Under Article 16, governments must provide financial assistance to families and children in the form of social security benefits. Such benefits must constitute an 'adequate income supplement for a significant number of families (although they may be subject to a means test)'. The Conservatives are clearly failing to meet this obligation, so Labour must stand up for families by, for instance, introducing a cap on private sector rents, repealing the Coalition's harshest policies (notably the 'bedroom tax'), and preventing the minimum income from falling any further. Although these changes will be costly, they are an important step towards reducing inequality and child poverty. This will save money in the longer term, while promoting Labour's core values of fairness and social justice.

Meanwhile, Article 17 includes a right to free primary and secondary education for all children, which must be both accessible and effective. This requirement builds on Article 16, according to which 'childcare services, particularly for infants, must exist in sufficient numbers to meet families' needs'. Additionally, these services must be affordable and of a high standard. Since 2010, however, funding for Sure Start has been reduced by approximately a third, leading to the closure or reduction of an estimated 400 centres. Unsurprisingly, it is the poorest families who are the worst affected, as Sure Start centres play a vital role in breaking the cycle of intergenerational poverty. Thus, Labour must commit itself once more to early-years investment by reinstating funding for Sure Start and setting up centres in areas where there are none at present. By doing so, it will improve outcomes for thousands of children while strengthening local communities.[13]

Like civil rights, these social and economic rights must be linked to their concomitant duties. Such obligations might include a responsibility to undertake paid employment, on the grounds that work is not only good for individual wellbeing and dignity, but also produces wider social and economic benefits. Similarly, people with disabilities should be encouraged to work if their condition allows it, but it is imperative that those who are unable to do so receive the support they need. However, the state must also value non-paid labour – such as parenting, caring and voluntary work – within the system. This aspect is neglected at present, and Labour should recognise the significant contribution that unpaid workers make to society.

The ESC also implies a number of obligations for the private sector. For instance, Article 2 upholds the right to just conditions of work; Article 3 enshrines the right to safe, healthy working conditions; and Article 4 guarantees the right to a fair remuneration sufficient for a decent standard of living for workers and their families. As such, Labour must take action to end the abuse of zero-hours contracts, and also make progress towards the introduction of a proper living wage. This would be an important step in tackling in-work poverty, which blights the lives of millions of people, while rectifying the injustice of low-paying employers relying on the state to top up pay through the benefits system. Thus, the living wage would save taxpayers' money, improve workers' morale and productivity, and boost company reputations by allowing them to market themselves as ethical employers.[14]

A commitment to the ESC, while in Opposition, would enable the Labour Party to mount a powerful challenge to the Conservatives' sustained assault on the most vulnerable people in society. On a return to government, the Charter would provide a blueprint for repairing the social safety net and tackling the injustices that have proliferated since 2010. The ESC would also place economic and social rights on an equal footing with civil and political rights, and thus redress the present constitutional imbalance between equality and liberty.[15] This is important because greater economic equality would make the liberties set out in the HRA more meaningful. After all, an individual cannot be truly free if they are unable to pay their rent or feed their family. The ESC thus has a crucial role to play in the creation of a fairer, more cohesive society, and Labour must make the case for its full incorporation into UK law.

Conclusion

This chapter has argued that Labour must champion civil liberties by reaffirming its traditional commitments to universal welfare entitlements and the protection of individuals from arbitrary state action. In policy terms, these principles suggest a three-pronged approach. First, Labour must work towards a better balance between liberty and security. This can be achieved not through increasingly draconian legislation, but by placing terrorism suspects within the criminal justice system and using existing powers to monitor their activities. Second, Labour needs to reaffirm its commitment to human rights. By pairing these rights with their concomitant responsibilities, the Party can foster civic duty and a sense of common citizenship. Third, Labour should enhance civil liberties by championing economic and social rights. This will enable it to tackle the problems of inequality and social exclusion, and thus improve the lives of Britain's most vulnerable citizens.

The approach presented in this chapter demands that Labour should mount a vigorous challenge against concentrations of power and vested interests. In particular, it must introduce stringent systems of checks and balances into all parts of the criminal justice system, and ensure that the private sector plays its part in addressing such issues as sustainable development and living standards. After all, there are limits on what individuals and the state can do alone, and a new framework of rights and duties is required to enforce corporate responsibility. This will not be easy but, in this age of fracking and food banks, it represents a vital step towards building a fairer, more just society.

Notes

[1] Labour Party, *Let Us Face the Future: A Declaration of Labour Policy for the Consideration of the Nation*, 1945, www.labour-party.org.uk/manifestos/1945/1945-labour-manifesto.shtml.

[2] Quoted in T. Jones, *Remaking the Labour Party: From Gaitskell to Blair* (London: Routledge, 1996), p 122.

[3] S. Driver and L. Martell, *New Labour* (Cambridge: Polity Press, 2006, 2nd edn), p 137; Charter 88, *The Original Charter 88*, 1988, www.unlockdemocracy.org.uk/?page_id=551.

[4] Driver and Martell, *New Labour*, p 142.

[5] P. Butler, 'Poverty – and child poverty in particular – is rising', *Guardian*, 29 April 2015, www.theguardian.com/society/2015/apr/29/poverty-child-rising-welfare-cuts-tory-claims.

[6] Bar Council, 'Bar Council warns over "double lock" safeguards in draft Investigatory Powers Bill', *Politics Home*, 4 November 2015, www.politicshome.com/document/press-release/bar-council/bar-council-warns-over- per centE2 per cent80 per cent9Cdouble-lock per centE2 per cent80 per cent9D-safeguards-draft; Liberty, *Liberty's Second Reading Briefing on the Terrorism Prevention and Investigative Measures Bill*, June 2011 available: http://www.liberty-human-rights.org.uk/pdfs/policy11/liberty-s-second-reading-briefing-on-the-terrorism-prevention-and-investigat.pdf, pp 4, 30–2, 34; A. Travis, 'Snooper's charter should be replaced by strengthening of existing powers', *Guardian*, 29 May 2013, www.

theguardian.com/world/2013/may/29/privacy-existing-powers-snoopers-charter; Liberty, 2011, pp 33–4.

[7] BBC News, *Spending Review: George Osborne Protects Police Funding*, 25 November 2015, www.bbc.co.uk/news/uk-34922126.

[8] Y. Cooper, *The Role for Government in Seeking to Ensure People's Liberty and Security*, 8 July 2013, www.labour.org.uk/role-for-government-in-seeking-to-ensure-liberty,2013-07-08.

[9] Ministry of Justice, *Rights and Responsibilities: Developing Our Constitutional Framework* Cm 7577 (Norwich: The Stationery Office Ltd, 2009), pp 8–10.

[10] Ministry of Justice, *Rights and Responsibilities*, pp 33, 9, 19–20.

[11] Ministry of Justice, *Rights and Responsibilities*, p 49.

[12] Joint Committee on Human Rights, *The Status of Economic, Social and Cultural Rights*, 2 November 2004, www.publications.parliament.uk/pa/jt200304/jtselect/jtrights/183/18307.htm.

[13] A. Grice, 'Pay up or watch child poverty get worse, top advisers tell coalition', *Independent*, 22 April 2013, www.independent.co.uk/news/uk/politics/pay-up-or-watch-child-poverty-get-worse-top-advisers-tell-coalition-8581997.html; Secretariat of the ESC, *Children's Rights under the European Social Charter*, date unknown, www.coe.int/t/dGHI/monitoring/Socialcharter/Theme per cent20factsheets/FactsheetChildren_en.pdf, pp 3, 9, 4; P. Butler, 'Hundreds of Sure Start Centres have closed since election, says Labour', *Guardian*, 28 January 2013, www.theguardian.com/society/2013/jan/28/sure-start-centres-closed-labour.

[14] P. Goyal, 'We should have the courage to legislate for a Living Wage, not just campaign for it', *Labour Uncut*, 18 April 2013, http://labour-uncut.co.uk/2013/04/18/we-should-have-the-courage-to-legislate-for-a-living-wage-not-just-campaign-for-it/.

[15] K. Ewing, 'Constitutional reform and human rights: Unfinished business?', *The Edinburgh Law Review* 5 (2001), pp 297–324.

SEVEN

Citizenship and the constitution

Emily Robinson[1]

Citizenship and the constitution

Shortly after his election as Labour Party leader, Jeremy Corbyn announced that the first pillar (of three) of his leadership would be 'the democratisation of public life from the ground up'. This 'new politics' would signal a sharp break from the practices of the New Labour governments. Corbyn talked about instituting 'a genuinely new political direction for the country', based on the 'thirst for a different kind of politics', which had been building not only in the Labour Party, but in the country. The instruments of this change were to be online democracy, citizens' assemblies, community control of local services and a constitutional convention examining the electoral system, House of Lords reform and the voting age.[2]

It is worth remembering that Tony Blair similarly began his leadership of the Labour Party with a promise to enact 'the biggest programme of change to democracy ever proposed by a political party'.[3] Thirteen years later, Gordon Brown pledged 'a new British constitutional settlement that entrusts more power to Parliament and the British people.'[4] For both – as for Corbyn – constitutional change was a way to signify a break with the abuses of the immediate past, and to demonstrate their commitment to good government and popular sovereignty. In Brown's case, of course, that immediate past was Blair's own period in office. Although a massive programme of constitutional change had indeed been enacted, by 2007 the need for democratic renewal seemed more urgent than ever. None materialised.

Corbyn comes from a strand within the Labour Party that has placed great stress on traditions of radical democracy. This takes a symbolic form, most obviously in its celebration of the historical ancestors, like the Levellers, and also a practical form, expressed through the desire to empower the Party's grassroots against its leadership. This is in stark contrast to the approach of Blair, who sidelined members in the interests of Party cohesion and electability. However, Blair's stance on constitutional reform must be understood against the background of Charter 88, which took much of its energy from long-standing attempts by the New Left to create a vigorous and participative democratic culture in Britain. Therefore, as Corbyn returns to this quest, it is worth examining the contradictions and obstacles against which previous attempts at reform have foundered.

Constitutional reform since 1997

Charter 88 channelled popular discontent with the governing party into a campaign for a complete overhaul of the British constitution, including the need to limit the power of the executive and to guarantee the rights of citizens in a written constitution. Its focus on the excesses of the Thatcher governments managed to bridge the gap between socialist and liberal reformers, which assisted with the creation of a 'progressive alliance' in the run up to the 1997 election. Although Blair was never a whole-hearted advocate of the Charter, his governments implemented three of its ten demands: freedom of information, an independent judiciary and the Human Rights Act. They also made significant inroads into two of the others by devolving power to Scotland, Wales and Northern Ireland and abolishing hereditary peerages. Attempts were also made to strengthen local and regional government and to empower individuals and communities through a series of radical experiments with participatory governance. In addition, more proportionate electoral systems were also introduced – if only outside Westminster. These reforms were so significant that Vernon Bogdanor has dubbed them Britain's 'new constitution'.[5] They have created lasting changes in political culture as well as constitutional structure – particularly in the relationship between the constituent nations of the United Kingdom.

Yet they did not add up to a coherent whole. Charter 88's thoroughgoing radicalism became a disparate series of constitutional innovations. Moreover, in too many cases, their original purpose was neutered by the desire to retain enough power at the centre to enact New Labour's social and economic policies. Much has been made of Blair's personal lack of interest in constitutional reform. He inherited commitments on devolution from John Smith, and ended up with the joint Lib-Dem/Labour consultative committee almost by accident, as the legacy of a pact he no longer needed. In particular, his enthusiasm for electoral reform evaporated in the face of the majority of 179 granted to him by the existing system. In turn, the goodwill of constitutional reformers also dried up. Blair was accused of hoarding the power he had promised to decentralise; of abusing the system he had set out to reform; and of alienating those he aimed to empower.

Brown's 2007 Green Paper on *The Governance of Britain* aimed to rectify this situation. The power of the executive would be severely curtailed in twelve areas, including the ability to deploy troops abroad, to dissolve and to recall Parliament, to ratify international treaties, to make public appointments and to control the civil service. In addition, the government's ability to spin would be restricted by simplifications to the reporting of government expenditure and a 24-hour limit on ministers' access to official statistics before publication. Finally, a series of proposals aimed to 're-invigorate democracy' and repair 'the relationship between the citizen and the state', through reforming the House of Lords, making local service providers accountable to citizens and requiring public bodies to involve local people in major decisions. Other topics highlighted for consultation included electoral reform, devolving budgets to local communities, weekend election days, and the right to protest outside Parliament. The eventual Constitutional Reform and Governance Act (2010) brought in only a fraction of these measures. It put the civil service on a statutory footing and provided for parliamentary approval of the ratification of treaties. Most of the rest had dissolved along the way.

The final year of Brown's premiership was dominated by the revelations of MPs' corrupt and excessive claims for expenses. This seemed to hasten the need for thorough reform. Progress, the centre-left pressure group, put forward a programme intended to grasp this 'once-in-a-lifetime chance, to make politics relevant again, to make Parliament matter once more, to make all of our people feel part of the governing of their own country and the running of their own communities.'[6] The centrepiece of this programme was the demand for a Citizens' Convention on Constitutional Reform, developed with campaign group Unlock Democracy, and rooted in a proposed Public Accountability and Political Ethics Bill. Yet, nothing happened. Once again, the 'once-in-a-lifetime chance' was missed.

This is hardly a problem specific to New Labour. Despite Nick Clegg's promise of the 'biggest shake-up' of democracy since the 1832 Reform Act, the actions of the Conservative–Liberal Democrat coalition were both limited and slow. The referendum on electoral reform was restricted to AV (and badly managed); the models used for e-petitions and the power to recall MPs were both designed to give little real power to citizens; the Transparency of Lobbying Act of 2014 was criticised by both campaigners and the Political and Constitutional Reform Committee as seriously flawed; House of Lords reform was very limited; and attempts to reform party funding came to nothing. The most substantial change – the introduction of fixed term parliaments – came about as a by-product of the need to stabilise the Coalition itself.

The localism promised by both Coalition partners also proved rather empty in practice. Limited schemes for engagement at community level were accompanied by central interference with the decisions of local authorities on everything from council tax to bin collection. Moreover, despite Conservative calls for a Big Society in which citizens are encouraged to take responsibility for the common good, the Coalition's policies proved both divisive and disempowering. The administration of Personal Independence Payments by Atos is only the most obvious example. Far from engendering a culture of trust and responsibility, the government treated too many of its citizens with suspicion and contempt.

As it becomes increasingly obvious that we are not 'all in this together', so it becomes more urgent to strengthen democratic processes and to deepen our conception of citizenship. Jeremy Corbyn's critique of New Labour and his commitment to tackling vested interests put him in an excellent position to reclaim this agenda, and Labour's own Constitutional Convention, established in autumn 2015 under Jon Trickett, could provide a solid basis for doing so. Yet, while this is laudable and sorely needed, it is worth taking a moment to ask what went wrong before. Why, despite all the good intentions of New Labour, all the groundwork laid by Charter 88 and others, all the significant constitutional reforms and the experiments with participative decision-making, why – despite all that – did we end up back where we started? Why are politicians still the least trusted profession, whom 79 per cent of us expect to lie?[7] Why do only 33 per cent of the public think that our political system works well? [8] And why is political participation still so strongly correlated with being older, white, affluent and male?[9]

What went wrong?

Both the Blair and Brown governments must take their share of the blame for this situation. Both were associated with spin and dishonesty, both prioritised electoral strategy over meaningful engagement with potential voters, and both failed in their attempts to revitalise Britain's tired political system. Yet there are wider reasons for the latter. Plans for political and constitutional reform fell foul of a series of obstacles, all four of which remain in place and must be confronted if any future reform programme is to succeed.

The first of these is the institutional tendency towards the status quo. The British system places an enormous amount of power in the hands of the executive, particularly when it is backed by a large parliamentary majority. To renounce or to limit that is difficult, especially as the system itself tends quite happily towards inertia. Any meaningful devolution of power or strengthening of constitutional checks requires resolution, persistence and – above all – a coherent strategy and reason for doing so. A general sense of the need to 'reinvigorate democracy' is not enough. The power of the centre can be seductive to any party, as the Thatcher governments testify: a party committed to breaking down the state ended up strengthening it beyond measure. However, this has always been particularly difficult for Labour.

This is the second obstacle, the fact that, as many scholars have noted, Labour has tended to be 'a constitutionally conservative party, not a radical one'.[10] This was not always the case. The popular democratic inheritance of Chartism continued to influence social democrats into the latter decades of the nineteenth century, inspiring demands for electoral reform, the abolition of the House of Lords and the monarchy and the institution of a republic based on direct participative democracy. However, this energy dissipated thereafter into a rather compromised acceptance of the state as it was. On the one hand this was a pragmatic Fabian preference for representative rather than participative democracy; on the other, it was the electoral imperative for Labour leaders to prove themselves responsible politicians. And once Labour found itself in a position to use the powers of the state in the cause of social justice, many of its parliamentarians became understandably resistant to weakening those powers.

The desire for outcomes, for measurable material change, is a constant preoccupation for social democrats. And rightly so. This is why the 'new localism' of the Blair years was always defined by strong minimum standards, measured through audits and targets and protected through ring-fenced budgets. This is how New Labour made its advancements in health and education. But it is also how it came to be characterised as managerial and statist. Mechanisms intended to devolve power ended up being used to centralise it. In particular, the government found itself unable to trust local democratic processes, preferring to by-pass local authorities and enable citizens to exercise (limited) choice over local health, housing, education and regeneration policies through schemes which were directly accountable to central government.[11]

There were three distinct rationales behind 'new localism', which tended to pull against rather than to reinforce one another. First, it was seen as a way to generate efficient public services, responsive to local needs. The main mechanisms for this were individual choice by service users – such as personal care budgets – and collective voice through consultation exercises. Second was the desire for democratic accountability and restoring faith in the formal political process. This led to the reform of local government structures in order to create visible figureheads – whether directly elected mayors, or visible cabinet members – with backbench councillors performing a 'community champion' role. Finally, there was the sense that participative and active citizenship was a good in itself, as argued by Robert Putnam, the American political scientist who became something of an inspiration for many of New Labour's thinkers. Putnam argued that active members of close-knit communities would be healthier, happier and safer.[12] This was the driving force behind the Civic Renewal Unit and the Active Citizenship Centre at the Home Office and it manifested itself in local participatory budgeting and citizens' juries, community-driven regeneration schemes like the New Deal for Communities and a range of small-scale experiments, including time banks and Local Exchange Trading Schemes.

Public engagement is hard to do. It is particularly hard to do equitably. When used as the basis for allocating public resources it bears a tremendous responsibility. Despite the best of intentions, it is difficult to avoid the conclusion that the first strand of thought – that localism was a means to generate efficient public services – ended up taking priority over the other two. We can see this particularly clearly in the case of Sure Start, where the radical devolution of control to parents in particular localities – apparently inspired by anarcho-syndicalism –

eventually gave way to the need to provide childcare on a consistent basis across the country.[13]

This brings us to the third obstacle, which is that Labour has never had to develop a theory of the state. Its struggle has been to be the representative of the people, their voice in Parliament. As a result, it still has difficulty seeing itself as part of the political establishment. This was particularly apparent in the surprise felt by many in the Party when independent mayors were elected in areas that had been one-party Labour strongholds for decades. While it may not be a comfortable thought, we must realise that, to most people, Labour represents 'the political class' far more than 'ordinary working people'. It is part of the establishment, of the vested interests, which voters need (and want!) to be empowered against. While Corbyn may appear more credible here than some, it is still a problem that he cannot ignore.

This is not only a barrier to Labour developing a workable reform programme; it is also a barrier to anything it does put forward being accepted. Distrust of politicians now runs so deep that anything proposed by a political party with the aim of enhancing democracy invites instant cynicism. We saw this, for instance, with the 2004 referendum for directly elected regional assemblies in the North East. Polls in 2002 showed that 72–73 per cent of respondents in the North East, North West, Yorkshire and the Humber and the West Midlands were in favour of elected regional assemblies, yet in the event 78 per cent of voters in the North East rejected the plans (on a 47.8 per cent turnout) and the government withdrew its plans elsewhere. It seems likely that the character of the Yes campaign itself – dominated by politicians including John Prescott – contributed to this reversal of opinion. The No campaign certainly played on public dislike of politicians by stoking up fears that this was a ruse to create more publicly-funded political posts.

The final obstacle is the sense that this is not – and should not be – a priority for socialists or social democrats. Questions of citizenship and constitutional reform often appear to be something of a luxury, nice so long as they don't impinge on other things, but really more the concern of Liberals than of true Labour politics. The implication is that those with time to worry about the nature of the constitution have few socio-economic problems on their plate. That may be true, but the well-documented crisis of participation, of trust in the democratic process and of engagement with formal politics, should concern social democrats more than anyone. First, because constitutional reform is about power and access to power: if social democracy is about anything it is about restructuring power relations. This is why radical democratic reform was so central to early socialism. Second, because political exclusion is intimately connected with social and economic exclusion. It is the poorest who participate the least. And third, because we believe in politics and collective decision-making as a means of solving problems. This requires a legitimate political process that carries the faith of its citizens. Without an expanded conception of citizenship and a truly democratic constitutional settlement, all other achievements run the risk of paternalism – of doing 'to' people what we believe is best.

Radical political reform

As Corbyn's speech made clear, the Labour Party needs to re-discover its commitment to radical political reform, to challenging vested interests and empowering the disempowered. This is not a distraction from the financial crisis; it is an essential part of any response to it. Vested interests cannot be separated into neat 'financial', 'political' and 'social' categories, as scandals about lobbying, tax avoidance, political donations and the granting of peerages continue to show. Outright anger over each scandal fades and can easily be channeled into another inquiry, another committee, another review. But distrust and cynicism remain and harden. It should be a point of principle for social democrats to tackle this and the system that engenders it. Moreover, it cannot be done from Westminster. The parties are all deeply embedded in this system, with conflicting sets of loyalties and priorities, as indicated by the recurring stalemate over party funding and over the recommendations of the Leveson Inquiry. A more radical solution is necessary, one which places responsibility and agency directly in the hands of citizens.

This will not be easy. In her book, *Talking to a Brick Wall*, Deborah Mattinson has described what she calls 'Peter Pan politics' in which the public refuse to take responsibility for democracy, believing this is the sole preserve of politicians but then blaming them for being out of touch.[14] Yet, it is clear that an appetite for greater involvement does exist. Since 2004 the Hansard Society has been measuring levels of knowledge of, satisfaction with, and participation in the political process through its annual *Audit of Political Engagement*. The 2016 report noted a marked improvement in people's propensity to say that they would vote and their belief that Parliament is essential to democracy – though it remains to be seen whether this will hold up in a non-election year. Forty-one per cent of respondents said that they would like to be very or fairly involved in national decision-making and 46 per cent in local decision making. However, their perception of their current ability to influence decisions was just 13 per cent at national level and 25 per cent locally.[15] There is clearly a gulf between people's willingness to participate and their current opportunities to do so. Yet this desire for influence does not translate straightforwardly into a desire for constitutional reform. Politicians are right when they say that this is not a question which comes up frequently on doorsteps. In 2013 the Hansard Society asked respondents to choose up to three suggestions for improving the British political system from a list of nine. Just 8 per cent chose 'Constitutional changes (for example, elected House of Lords, different voting system)' as one of their three, fewer than the 11 per cent who said 'none of the above'. Yet greater transparency (48 per cent), greater accountability (39 per cent) and more citizen participation in decision-making (29 per cent) were all popular choices.[16]

It is also apparent that current attempts to resolve the problems of our political system may actually be deepening them. For instance, the No. 10 e-Petitions website, first established in 2006 and reformed and re-launched in both 2011 and 2015, has been very popular. Between 2011 and 2012 36,000 petitions were submitted and a total of 6.4 million signatures recorded – an average of 12 a minute. The attraction is obvious. It allows voters to make their voices heard on issues they care about, with little commitment on their part and no requirement to engage in complex or difficult decision-making. It has been labelled 'megaphone democracy'. However, campaigners including the Hansard Society and Unlock Democracy have questioned the extent to which it really does enable petitioners' voices to be heard. Only those petitions which pass the threshold of 100,000 signatures are granted the possibility of being debated in Parliament and even those which reach that stage can be dismissed with little real discussion at all. Natascha Engel, former Chair of the backbench business committee – which considers the petitions up for debate – has warned that the gap between what the petitions system promises and what it actually delivers risks alienating voters still further. In her words, 'this is not public engagement. This is just making people angry with politicians.'[17]

The perception that politicians are 'all the same', 'in it for themselves' and 'not to be trusted' damages all parties' efforts in all policy areas, but it should be of particular concern to social democrats. It is impossible to achieve the necessary mandate for transformative social and economic policies if the public has no faith in either the system as a whole or in Labour as a party. This is an opportunity for us to take the lead, to build a new consensus for reform.

Labour citizens

One crucial first step is for Labour to treat its own members and supporters as citizens, as collaborators in a joint enterprise. We already know this. And the Party has been struggling to find a way to act upon it for at least three decades. While the experience of allowing registered supporters to vote for the Party leadership was controversial, it did at least provide an opportunity to rethink the boundaries of Labour's demos and its relationship with sympathisers outside the Party's walls.[18] Corbyn's stated desire to be 'open to the people we seek to represent... giving them a voice through our organisation and policy-making' is a good first step. He recognised that this means 'remak[ing] our Party as a real social movement...rooted in our communities'.[19] However, it is vital that this is about more than mobilising those who are already engaged in anti-austerity politics. We need to attract people who know more about the communities they come from than they do about political activism. Labour needs to become a party *of* and *by* the people again – not simply *for* them. An obvious way to do this is through well-publicised local recruitment campaigns for candidates and public hustings with open primary elections. This should not be seen as disempowering local members, but as strengthening them in relation to the national Party. They should be the driving force of a strong politics of place, rooted in the concerns and identities of particular localities, not just the ground-troops of centrally directed campaigns.

The national Party can also do far more to open up. Since his election as Party leader, Corbyn has been experimenting with various ways of doing this, most obviously through his approach to Prime Minister's Questions. He has also suggested allowing members to vote in indicative online ballots throughout the year.[20] In summer 2013 Neal Lawson suggested that Labour should allow Party members to decide its campaign priorities, using online petitioning, and also that it should open a day of its annual conference to the public so that the leadership can 'listen to people telling them what they think of their form of politics'.[21] The obvious objection is that by opening itself to public opinion in this way, Labour will become (in Tony Benn's memorable phrase), a weathervane rather than a signpost. But hearing and giving voice to the concerns of ordinary citizens should always be Labour's primary purpose. And that means listening to the questions which citizens pose to Labour, as well as to their opponents. Yes, it needs to place these concerns within a solid framework of social democratic principles and, of course, it will often have to say 'No'. But it also can and should participate in a mature and responsible conversation with members and supporters about where the Party is heading, what its priorities should be and where it will take the country when it returns to government. And this must begin with a genuine desire to hear – and to consider – their views and experiences.

A citizens' convention

The next step is for Labour to recognise that it is part of the problem, to accept that any attempt to reform the political system must be free from the considerations of party politics.

This is why a formal Citizens' Convention on political reform, appointed by lot and distinct from the Party's own policy-making procedures, is the best proposal on offer. Its findings would be publicised and discussed in a series of public debates and its recommendations put to a referendum. Parties would of course be free to campaign, but should not have any privileged role in the decision-making process. It would remove the suspicion of partisan bias and the stultifying need for either intra- or inter-party agreement on any one issue. It would also allow the time and space for disinterested deliberation in a way that the usual forms of political negotiation – or referenda without deliberation, as with AV in 2011 or the EU in 2016 – cannot. Unlike the disjointed reforms of the Blair years, the Convention would be tasked with examining the entire system and the legal, philosophical and cultural assumptions on which it stands. Its recommendations would be developed in tandem with one another and put to the public in one piece. Even if no changes were recommended, this would be based on a considered account of what our constitution does and how it does it.

The most important requirement is that the Convention should not be restricted in its remit, but free to enquire into all aspects of our political system, from top to bottom. It would be up to the members of the Convention – and ultimately the electorate – to decide on the proper relationship between the tiers of government; between the legislative and the executive; and between representative and participative forms of democracy. The topics suggested in 2009 by Progress and Unlock Democracy were the reform of the House of Lords and of the House of Commons, including strengthening Select Committees and making the Executive more accountable; party funding; electoral reform; primary elections and directly elected mayors; and greater devolution of power, accountability and funding to local government. These topics are a good place to start, if perhaps rather tied to the longstanding concerns of what is sometimes called the 'democracy movement'. Crucially, the members of the Convention should be free to shape the agenda as they see fit. It seems unlikely that they would ignore questions of lobbying, corporate accountability and media ownership; an economic and social bill of rights might even make an appearance.

The Convention should also be granted unlimited access to information, evidence and expert opinions. They should be able to scrutinise even the most secret aspects of the constitution, including, for instance, the role of the royal family. This is a good example of a topic on which it has always been difficult for Labour to form a consistent opinion. The Party's commitment to equality of opportunity and aversion to the hereditary principle has tended to fade beside the (possibly ill-founded) suspicion that republicanism is not a vote-winner. The media treatment of Corbyn's agonies on this issue has seemed to confirm these fears. Yet at the very least, this is a topic which would benefit from greater public scrutiny.

A Citizens' Convention would allow such complex and divisive topics to be thoroughly aired and considered away from the demands of electoral politics. The Labour Party is likely find itself divided on this issue, and on many of the others that may come before the Convention. But it would only be required to commit to full scrutiny, open deliberation and a free public vote; the rest would be in the hands of the British people.

Conclusion

A Citizens' Convention on political reform is certainly not guaranteed to reform the political process – or to restore people's faith in it – overnight. It may achieve very little at all. However, it would go some way to addressing all four of the obstacles to reform identified in this chapter. First, by establishing a clear process and timetable, outside the normal structures of Westminster, it would be less likely to be overcome by institutional inertia than previous attempts. Second, it would be able to concentrate on questions of democracy and accountability, free of the conflicting pressures of other policy priorities. Third, it would accept that political parties are themselves part of the problem and that deliberation about the democratic process must be separated from the influence of immediate electoral concerns. And finally, it would make clear once and for all that empowering citizens *is* a priority for social democrats and that this principle lies at the heart of everything we believe.

A manifesto commitment to introduce a formal Citizens' Convention on political reform would be a big, bold statement. It would demonstrate that Labour is not only willing to reform our political system, but – unlike in 1997 – to let go of the process, to devolve decision-making on the biggest questions of all to citizens. And that Convention would stand the best chance yet of reforming our messy, knotty, opaque system in a way that retains the sympathy of the British people – and is able to regain their trust.

Notes

[1] I am grateful to Matt Beech and Paul Richards for comments on a previous draft of this article, to Kevin Hickson for organising this edited collection, and to the members of the Social Democratic Philosophy Group for advice and encouragement over a number of years.

[2] Jeremy Corbyn, Labour Party South West Region conference, 21 November 2015, http://press.labour.org.uk/post/133652381834/speech-by-jeremy-corbyn-mp-leader-of-the-labour.

[3] Tony Blair, Labour Party Conference, 4 October 1994.

[4] Gordon Brown, 3 July 2007.

[5] V. Bogdanor, *The New British Constitution* (Oxford: Hart, 2009).

[6] B. Brivati, 'Introduction', in L. Baston, B. Brivati, M. Cain, D. Finch et al, *Real Reform Now: Why Progressives Should Embrace Democratic Renewal and How We Get There* (London: Progress, 2009), p 6.

[7] Ipsos MORI, 'Politicians are still trusted less than estate agents, journalists and bankers', 22 January 2016, www.ipsos-mori.com/researchpublications/researcharchive/3685/Politicians-are-still-trusted-less-than-estate-agents-journalists-and-bankers.aspx.

[8] Hansard Society, *Audit of Political Engagement 13: The 2015 Report* (London: Hansard Society, 2016).

[9] Hansard Society, *Audit of Political Engagement 13*.

[10] V. Bogdanor, *Power and the People: A Guide to Constitutional Reform* (London: Weidenfeld and Nicolson, 1997), p 112. See also P. Dorey, *The Labour Party and Constitutional Reform: A History of Constitutional Conservatism* (Basingstoke: Palgrave, 2008) and L. Barrow and I. Bullock, *Democratic Ideas and the British Labour Movement, 1880–1914* (Cambridge: Cambridge University Press, 1996).

[11] G. Lodge and R. Muir, 'Localism under New Labour', *Political Quarterly* 81 (2010), pp S96–S107.

[12] R. Putnam, *Bowling Alone: The Collapse and Revival of American Community* (New York: Simon and Schuster, 2000).

[13] N. Glass, 'Surely some mistake?' *Guardian*, 5 January 2005, www.theguardian.com/society/2005/jan/05/guardiansocietysupplement.childrensservices.

[14] D. Mattinson, *Talking to a Brick Wall: How New Labour Stopped Listening to the Voter and Why We Need a New Politics* (London: BiteBack, 2010).

[15] Hansard Society, *Audit of Political Engagement 13*.

[16] Hansard Society, *Audit of Political Engagement 10: The 2013 Report* (London: Hansard Society, 2013).

[17] N. Engel, 'Why the E-petitions system isn't working', *Guardian*, Comment is Free, 16 November 2011, www.theguardian.com/commentisfree/2011/nov/16/e-petitions-system.

[18] J. Garland, 'A wider range of friends: Multi-speed organising during the 2015 Labour leadership contest', *Political Quarterly* 87, 1 (2015), pp 23–30.

[19] Jeremy Corbyn, Labour Party South West Region conference, 21 November 2015.

[20] Jeremy Corbyn, Labour Party South West Region conference, 21 November 2015

[21] N. Lawson, quoted in J. Harris, 'Where is Labour going wrong?', *Guardian*, 11 August 2013, www.theguardian.com/commentisfree/2013/aug/11/where-labour-going-wrong-ed-miliband.

EIGHT

Internationalism

Matt Beech[1]

The Labour tradition is both internationalist and patriotic.[2] To its detriment patriotism is an under-used term in the lexicon of the British centre-left but internationalism remains. While patriotism deeply values and cherishes the hallmarks of one's own nation, internationalism speaks of the virtue of transcending national borders and domestic concerns. On the one hand internationalism is about cooperation with other nation-states for mutual benefit such as trade agreements. On the other hand, it requires a collective view of global problems including an acute awareness of social injustice and an acknowledgement of the innumerable human rights violations which occur daily on each continent. Internationalism in the Labour tradition is underpinned more than anything else by the ancient truth that people, regardless of creed, religion or nationality, share innate moral worth bound by common humanity. Parts of the Labour movement struggle with patriotism. The New Left understood it as an emotional hangover from Britain's imperial past. Some on the Labour right, self-styled 'progressives', deem it as a proclivity of the conservative mind. For other Labour politicians it is conspicuous by its absence; an unuttered sentiment that is best confined to the Party's history. Here is the disconnect. Labour voters are comfortable with patriotism while its activists are less so. Like so many contemporary issues there is a divergence between citizens whose instinct is to vote Labour and die-hard politicos who pound the pavements in all weathers. This is a significant problem because Labour MPs are drawn from its activist base. While they have dedication and ambition they speak not for Labour voters on a number of issues. This is especially the case in England where Labour is socially, economically and culturally disparate. One need look no further than how the Brexit debate divided great swathes of Labour voters whose instinct was to vote to leave against the mainstay of its activists and MPs who voted to remain inside the European Union.

The truth is that most Labour voters are proud of the United Kingdom. They feel British and English, or Welsh or Scottish. Like most people they are aware that they are fortunate to live and raise their children in a democratic, free, nation-state. They are proud of English parliamentary tradition and common law liberties which have in great measure authored our British civic life. They are proud of what Labour governments have achieved at home and abroad: including the welfare state, NHS, national parks, the Open University, the national minimum wage, tax credits, decolonisation, NATO, overseas aid and debt relief to developing nations.

The purpose of this chapter is to sketch an argument for Labour's internationalism that is also patriotic. By internationalism I mean to refer to Labour's global view. It speaks to the need for a fuller perspective of Britain's place in the world that walks closely in Labour traditions while acknowledging the challenges of the contemporary age. The first task of this chapter is to assess recent Labour history in terms of internationalism. The second task is to understand what internationalism – as Labour's global view – could mean in practice.

Labour's internationalism since 1997

The Blair governments in many ways fulfilled the aspirations of Labour voters in the field of internationalism. They came to office in a period of economic expansion in a relatively benign era when the afterglow of the cold war victory by the west could still be felt. When contrasted with today's acute and persistent threat from Wahhabi Islamic terrorists, and global economic uncertainty, New Labour's arrival at the apex of British politics was a different age. The majority of Blair's Cabinet had never served in government, and though he would become internationally known as a foreign policy Prime Minister, he possessed no prior government experience and in Opposition had never held the Shadow Foreign Secretary brief. In fact the UK had a young Prime Minister and a relatively untested cabinet.

Instinctively, the Blair governments were outward facing across the English Channel and the North Atlantic Ocean. The lens of globalisation was used to explain and understand Britain's future. This vision was facilitated by a liberal market economy and a preference for a flexible, mobile workforce from within and without the United Kingdom. The origin and problems of mass migration from European Union member states started here. New Labour's economic strategy was to use the proceeds of growth from an expanding economy to reinvest in public services and benefits. Hindsight reveals their approach to economics and public policy as a concoction of Labourist and Thatcherite assumptions.

When the public purse was loosened after two years of fiscal rectitude, the Comprehensive Spending Review of 1999 set the parameters for an historic programme of public investment. The Foreign and Commonwealth Office, the Ministry of Defence and the newly established Department for International Development were among the beneficiaries. New Labour committed national treasure and effort in pursuing internationalism and at the heart of it were the successes of the Kyoto Protocol, the Millennium Development Goals, Jubilee 2000, Responsibility to Protect (R2P), and various campaigns to extend universal human rights. They did this because, in Blair and Brown, the centre left had leaders who viewed Britain as a necessary force for good in the world.

Without ignoring New Labour's failings including their greatest sin – the 2003 Iraq War – the liberty of many Kosovan Albanian Muslims, citizens of Sierra Leone and Afghanistan was profoundly improved (if not fully safeguarded in the case of Afghanistan). As Blair famously said in relation to NATO bombing of Serbia in the Kosovan War:

> This is a just war, based not on any territorial ambitions but on values. We cannot let the evil of ethnic cleansing stand. We must not rest until it is reversed. We have learned twice before in this century that appeasement does not work. If we let an evil dictator range unchallenged, we will have to spill infinitely more blood and treasure to stop him later.[3]

Later in his 'Chicago Speech' he sums up his internationalism:

> We are all internationalists now, whether we like it or not. We cannot refuse to participate in global markets if we want to prosper. We cannot ignore new political ideas in other counties if we want to innovate. We cannot turn our backs on conflicts and the violation of human rights within other countries if we want still to be secure. On the eve of a new Millennium we are now in a new world. We need new rules for international cooperation and new ways of organising our international institutions.[4]

New Labour's internationalism committed blood as well as treasure to cross borders to secure human rights. This was a decisive break in British foreign policy. It can be seen as the introduction of humanitarian intervention into the internationalist doctrine as opposed to merely diplomacy and humanitarian aid. Britain's national interest was evolving and being defined more broadly. This corresponded with the end of the bi-polar international order, and the emergence of a multi-polar one, nonetheless dominated by the United States. The Blair governments elected that the UK would be a prolific actor in the multipolar international system of the post-cold war. Domestically, New Labour reclaimed the Union flag and the mantle of 'defenders of the realm' from the Conservative Party and invested in hard and soft power assets.

When Brown became Prime Minister he continued in many of the policy areas of his predecessor. The pall of Iraq's bloody civil war hung heavy around the British government. To this day, its shadow influences foreign policy discussion, planning and operations. In the aftermath of deposing Saddam Hussein and through the de-Ba'athification of Iraq's military, civil service and security sector, conflict raged on destabilising the region. The Taleban continued their stubborn rearguard action against western forces across Afghanistan, determined to wait out the 'infidels' and, inflict as much damage as possible to patrolling infantryman through Improvised Explosive Devices (IEDs). As Brown stated in his first Party Conference speech as Labour Leader:

> Because we will do our duty and discharge our obligations, we will work in Iraq and Afghanistan for three objectives: security, political reconciliation and economic reconstruction, and at all times we will do everything to ensure the security of our dedicated armed forces. Let me say: there should be no safe haven, no hiding place anywhere in the world for Al Qaeda and terrorism. To prevail in this struggle will require more than military force and we will work with our allies to isolate extremism and win the battle of hearts and minds.[5]

While New Labour's focus was on Iraq and Afghanistan little action other than financial aid and formal condemnation was given to atrocities occurring in Darfur, Sudan. Civil war, genocide and mass rape of non-Arab Africans, and huge displacement of citizens were the markers, of arguably, the greatest humanitarian crisis of the new century. Western sanctions continued against Zimbabwe as a formal means of conveying displeasure and disdain though countless Zimbabweans continued to suffer corruption, poverty and abuse under Robert Mugabe's long-time Zanu PF regime.

Ed Miliband's election and subsequent leadership of the Labour Party was notable in terms of Labour's internationalism for a number of reasons. First, he stated that the Iraq War was wrong and that Labour needed to move on:

Iraq was an issue that divided our Party and our country. Many sincerely believed that the world faced a real threat. I criticise nobody faced with making the toughest of decisions and I honour our troops who fought and died there. But I do believe that we were wrong. Wrong to take Britain to war and we need to be honest about that. Wrong because that war was not a last resort, because we did not build sufficient alliances and because we undermined the United Nations.[6]

Second, under Miliband Labour voted against a Conservative–Liberal coalition motion to conduct airstrikes in Syria against the regime of President Bashar Al-Assad. This was in direct response to Assad deploying chemical weapons – missiles of sarin gas – to kill hundreds of civilians in the district of Ghouta, Damascus. In his statement to the House of Commons during the debate Miliband concluded:

Let me end by saying this: the continued turmoil in the country and the region in the recent months and years further demonstrate the need for stability across the region – to protect the innocent civilians involved, and uphold the national interest and the security and future prosperity of the whole region and world. I am sure the whole House recognises that this will not and cannot be achieved through a military solution.[7]

Labour was not, in principle, against military action. They desired more time for the UN weapons inspectorate to gain the burden of proof required and to build a consensus, where practically possible, on the UN Security Council. Miliband's main argument was that the Conservative–Liberal coalition was proposing rushing into military action which could quickly turn into mission-creep and the United Kingdom could find itself embroiled in the Syrian civil war. Miliband was desperately trying to learn the lessons from the ill-conceived justifications of the Iraq War and this was in tune with the view of many Labour activists. However, it is arguable that the fear of the charge of heavy-handed interventionism and 'British imperialism' led to Her Majesty's government being denied its foreign policy which specifically sought to prevent further war crimes by the Assad regime. In the weeks that followed the UN weapons inspectorate confirmed the Assad regime's use of sarin gas in the Ghouta massacre. Third, under Miliband the 'Chicago Speech' doctrine of humanitarian intervention was relegated to the bottom of the list in the foreign policy thinking of the Labour Party. A lack of confidence and a more sceptical view of what can be achieved by hard power options dominated the 2010–15 period. Interestingly, it is during this same period that ISIS emerged as the most pervasive threat to human rights across the Middle East and in other regions of the world through their supporters (both formal and informal). It is accurate to say that in this period ISIS were and still continue to be the UK's most clear and present threat. Under Miliband Labour's reticence towards hard power did not extend to the defence of the realm and Labour continued to be supportive of the British state utilising the security services to protect its own citizens from jihad by Wahhabi Islamic terrorists.

Fourth, Labour's internationalism exhibited an unalloyed view of the free movement of people. It was not until the general election campaign of 2015 that some recognition of the sub-optimal effect of mass immigration on working-class communities finally surfaced. This was too little too late for a great many erstwhile Labour voters. They did not believe that Labour under Miliband (like Labour under Brown and Blair before him) thought that mass immigration from eastern and south-eastern Europe had been anything other than a boon for GDP. Along with disgruntled Conservatives (and surprisingly some Liberal Democrat voters) swathes of urban, working-class Labour voters comprised the 3.88 million votes cast for the UK Independence Party (UKIP) on 7 May 2015. Labour and the Conservative Party breathed a collective sigh of relief and thanked the First-Past-the-Post electoral system when those near 4 million UKIP votes translated, in typically perverse fashion, into a solitary parliamentary seat.

Jeremy Corbyn was elected Labour leader in September 2015 in the light of Labour's general election defeat. Corbyn is Labour's fourth leader in eight years. He is the most unlikely Labour leader in the Party's history as he only secured enough nominations moments before the ballot closed and through the generosity of MPs who never intended to vote for him. His place in the contest was due to a notion that a broad ideological debate was required. Corbyn's victory was overwhelming and Labour elected its most radical leader in the post-war era.

Corbyn, a veteran Bennite MP, is known for his knowledge of, and concern for, issues of foreign and defence policy and human rights. A complete appreciation of Labour's internationalism under Corbyn is not possible at this stage as a full raft of policies is yet to be presented. He has made it clear that he will not campaign to renew the Vanguard class of submarines which contain Trident nuclear missiles. This is consistent with his longstanding membership of the Campaign for Nuclear Disarmament (CND). Support for such a change to Labour's internationalism is not insignificant among activists and the Labour leadership has, in the past, advocated nuclear disarmament. Michael Foot famously fought the 1983 general election on a platform of unilateral nuclear disarmament.

The most high profile internationalist issue since becoming Party Leader has been Corbyn's decision to lead Labour against the Conservative government's motion of airstrikes against ISIS in Syria. After some argument within the Parliamentary Labour Party Corbyn permitted his MPs a free vote and on 2 December 2015 the House of Commons voted 397 to 223 for the government motion. While the vast majority of his MPs (152) followed their Leader's position 66 MPs voted with the government. During the debate on bombing ISIS targets Corbyn stated:

And the rejection of fourteen years of disastrous wars in the wider Middle East was a central pillar of the platform on which I was elected Labour Leader. In the light of that record western military interventions, UK bombing of Syria risks yet more of what President Obama called 'unintended consequences'. The spectre of Iraq, Afghanistan and Libya looms over this debate.

To oppose another reckless and half-baked intervention isn't pacifism. It's hard-headed common sense.[8]

Significant interventions from 'Labour rebels' came from Dame Margaret Beckett and Alan Johnson but the most commanding speech came from Labour's Shadow Foreign Secretary Hilary Benn who argued:

As a Party we have always been defined by our internationalism. We believe we have a responsibility one to another. We never have – and we never should – walk by on the other side of the road. And we are here faced by fascists. Not just their calculated brutality, but their belief that they are superior to every single one of us in this chamber tonight, and the people we represent. They hold us in contempt. They hold our values in contempt. They hold our belief in tolerance and decency in contempt. They hold our democracy, the means by which we will make our decision tonight, in contempt. And what we know about fascists is that they need to be defeated.'[9]

What is known about Corbyn's internationalism is that it is one critical of humanitarian intervention. His voting record on this is instructive. He voted against NATO bombing of Serbia in the Kosovan War in 1999 and against the Gaddafi regime in Libya in 2011. Corbyn's internationalism employs a heterodox reading of British national interests, which can be seen in his role as a longstanding critic of NATO – the cornerstone of European defence – which he has argued should be disbanded. This sits neatly with his criticism of American global power and foreign policy. He voted against military action against the Afghan Taleban after the 11 September 2001 terror attacks and against the Iraq War in 2003.

Corbyn hosted Sinn Fein leaders Gerry Adams and Martin McGuiness at the House of Commons in 1984 when they were regarded as *personae non gratae* by the British state, argued that British troops should be withdrawn from Northern Ireland, and has specifically refused to condemn IRA violence, including murders. As a member of the Palestine Solidarity Campaign one can expect that Corbyn believes in a separate homeland, a sovereign state for Palestinians. But what is highly controversial is Corbyn's willingness to use his political profile to arrange to speak and share platforms with members of proscribed terrorist organisations, namely Hamas and Hezbollah.

In Corbyn, Labour have a principled and radical socialist leader who has spent his long parliamentary career challenging the accepted orthodoxies of British foreign and defence policy. The problem for Labour is that much of the electorate are aware of this and deem Corbyn's internationalism to be a bar to holding the Office of Prime Minister.

Labour's global view in practice

What, in the contemporary age, should Labour's global view for the UK entail? The answer to this question involves two further questions: what is the UK's capacity to act internationally and what is its appetite to act internationally? First, with regards to capacity the UK is a permanent member of the United Nations Security Council and is considered powerful in diplomatic terms. As the fifth largest economy and a member of the G20 the UK is regarded as a significant power in economic terms. As a bearer of thermo-nuclear weapons the UK is deemed to be a nuclear power in military terms. Add to this the global reach of British values, culture, institutions and ideas and one can reasonably suggest that the UK is notable nation-state in terms of soft power. The fifth and final facet of the UK's power is its reputational influence which is predicated on the sum total of its behaviour in the minds of other members of the international community. Though it must be said that this facet is deeply contested by the hard-left and the hard-right. When these five facets of capacity are aggregated a case can be made that the UK is among a small number of *great powers*.

Second, with regards to the UK's appetite to act as a global leader the worldview of Her Majesty's government is the key variable, followed by the majority view of the Parliamentary Party of the government.

Public opinion is a highly important variable but one which can be often shaped. In general, the British public and Labour voters have come to expect the British state to be an active player in international affairs and have supported or demonstrated their acquiescence over humanitarian interventions and wars of self-defence. The UK's position is subordinate to the United States as the world's pre-eminent nation-state and superpower but, as a *great power* expected to fulfil responsibilities within the international community, its capacity and appetite for internationalism is beyond doubt.

What is clear is that Labour needs an appropriate form of internationalism so that the UK plays its role as a force for good in the world. A form of internationalism which harnesses soft and hard power assets and yet is rooted in a tradition of patriotism. What follows is a brief set of suggestions for Labour in defence, foreign and international aid policy.

Defence of the realm

Labour's defence of the realm requires NATO to retain the UK's chief defensive alliance from threats on Europe's eastern and south-eastern borders. To guarantee the defence of British interests and assets an elite maritime posture is demanded and to this end an increase in Royal Naval personnel and financial investment is required. Such investments would be sufficient to develop and staff a third aircraft carrier, a new generation of flexible combat vessels, expansion of the Royal Fleet Axillary and maintenance of the Astute class of attack submarines. In a nuclear world the UK requires the renewal of its Vanguard class submarines with Trident nuclear missiles as Britain's ultimate deterrent against hostile nuclear states.

To combat enemies within, and without, Labour's defence of the realm must continue the 'five-eyes' network of intelligence gathering and sharing between Britain's closest allies. All foreign nationals convicted of terror offences in the UK should be deported to their country of residence and the age of entry to the armed services should be raised to 18.

Foreign affairs

Labour's foreign policy should be one which seeks to exercise British national interests. Chief of which is to keep the UK as a *great power* and a leader in international affairs. It is in Britain's national interest to maintain our relationship with United States of America as our primary alliance and to continue our close strategic and defensive relationship with France as the other European *great power*. It is in our national interest to destroy ISIS and its allies where they are found; to protect eastern Europe from Russian expansionism and to deepen our diplomatic relationship with the People's Republic of China to encourage further trade and Chinese human rights.

International aid and development

Labour's international aid and development policy should keep the budget as 0.7 per cent of GDP and then to target investment of the budget in fewer areas giving priority to particular projects. These would include clean water, prevention of childhood diseases, female education, contraception and anti-retroviral drugs, English language and numeracy provision, education to prevent female genital mutilation, programmes to secure religious liberty, projects to protect refugees, grants for sustainable energy, construction of highways and rail networks.

Conclusion

For Labour, internationalism should not be an abstract principle, but one bonded to patriotism. Internationalism should not be pursued in isolation of the democratic will of the four nations of the United Kingdom. Straining towards an unconsidered internationalism leads to a transnational centre-left, rootless and unaware of the values of those for whom it claims to speak. By the same token, without a global view Labour patriotism can become insular. There is no obvious solution to Labour's differences on the issue of patriotism and the effect it has on the type of internationalism pursued. It is like two sides of a large family aware of their shared lineage but baffled by their contrasting dispositions. Labour's variance is a clash of identity and culture. It is the cosmopolitan against the heartlands.

What a future Labour government ought to do is to root its internationalism in the patriotic tradition of its past. Labour voters are proud when the United Kingdom protects the vulnerable and confronts tyranny. Be that in the form of Nazi Fascism, Soviet Communism, Irish paramilitarism (Republican and Loyalist), or in the present terrorist threat of Wahhabi Islamic fundamentalism. The focus of this admiration is often the men and women of the armed services who discharge the instructions of Her Majesty's government to defend the realm at home and abroad. Such a rootedness guards against the drift away from the values of Labour's soul, the communities through which its identity and ethos have been formed for more than a century. The need to measure the UK's capacity and understand the appetite of its citizens is as vital as the twin impulses of national interest and humanitarianism. Labour requires a global view for the UK, one that recognises it as a *great power*, and a global leader. A patriotic internationalism is the right prescription for the twenty-first century.

Notes

[1] I am grateful to my colleague Dr Christopher Martin for conversations about the defence of the realm during the writing of this essay. Any errors are my own.

[2] An exemplar of Labour patriotism from within the Labour Party is E.F.M. Durbin, *What Have We to Defend?* (London: Labour Book Service, 1942) and from a socialist non-member see G. Orwell, *The Lion and the Unicorn: Socialism and the English Genius* (London: Secker and Warburg, 1941).

[3] T. Blair, *Doctrine of the International Community*, Speech to the Economic Club, Chicago, 24 April 1999, http://webarchive.nationalarchives.gov.uk/+/www.number10.gov.uk/Page1297.

[4] Blair, *Doctrine*.

[5] G. Brown, Speech to the Labour Party Conference, Bournemouth, 24 September 2007, http://news.bbc.co.uk/1/hi/uk_politics/7010664.stm.

[6] E. Miliband, Speech to the Labour Party Conference, Manchester, 28 September 2010, www.bbc.co.uk/news/uk-politics-11426411.

[7] E. Miliband, Statement on Syria to the House of Commons, House of Commons, 29 August 2013, www.newstatesman.com/politics/2013/08/ed-milibands-commons-statement-syria-full-text.

[8] J. Corbyn, Speech against military action against ISIS in Syria, House of Commons, 2 December 2015, www.newstatesman.com/politics/staggers/2015/12/jeremy-corbyns-speech-against-military-action-against-isis-syria.

[9] H. Benn, Speech on military action against ISIS in Syria, House of Commons, 2 December 2015, www.newstatesman.com/politics/uk/2015/12/watch-hilary-benns-remarkable-speech-favour-air-strikes-syria.

NINE

Conclusion

Kevin Hickson

At this stage there can be no definitive answers as to how the Labour Party wins the next general election, or even if it can win, especially if there is a snap autumn poll following the appointment of the new Tory Leader and Prime Minister, Theresa May in July 2016. There is plenty of debate still between social democrats, or democratic socialists, over the future direction of the Party, just as there is in the pages of this book. As stressed in the Introduction the chapters contained in this book are the views of each individual author. What unites them is a belief that social democracy is still something worth fighting for and that in order to succeed there is a need to go back to the foundations of our ideology.

Arguably, there are four dilemmas which the Labour Party needs to face if it is to move forward.

The first of these is *leadership*. Although not addressed directly in the pages of this book, as the focus is on concepts rather than personalities, it is a crucial factor in winning elections. The leadership issue was a problematic one for Labour post-2010. Ed Miliband was elected largely, but not exclusively, on the votes of the trade unions and because he offered a clearer alternative to New Labour than the other candidates – with the exception of Diane Abbott, who never really was considered seriously. However, his tendency – or perhaps more the tendency of Shadow Chancellor Ed Balls – to advocate limited austerity meant that the electorate were confused as to what the Labour Party stood for, even as late as 2015. His defeat led some to call for a return to the politics of New Labour writ large but obviously the winning emotion in the 2015 leadership contest was the need for a clear alternative to austerity which only Jeremy Corbyn offered. Corbyn now has the overwhelming support of the grassroots but not of the Parliamentary Party. Clearly one issue was seeking to find common ground between the leadership and the PLP, something that appeared further away than ever after the decision to leave the EU. Corbyn has created the space for a reformulation of policy and ideas, moving on decisively from the era of New Labour.

Economic credibility – the key factor in explaining Labour's 2015 general election defeat is the loss of economic credibility in the banking crisis of 2008. As I stress in my own chapter in this book the relationship between economic performance and economic credibility is not straightforward. There were very real signs that the economy was starting to grow again by 2010, but Labour's reputation for economic competence that had been so hard to establish after the 'Winter of Discontent' had been lost. As Peter Hain stresses in his Foreword to this volume, George Osborne attacked the Labour government for running up the debt and the deficit and not planning to pay it down quickly enough. The result of Conservative–Lib Dem austerity was to choke off the growth that was present in 2010 with the result that by this year the deficit is actually higher than it would have been had Labour won and implemented its slower deficit reduction package. However, Labour's reputation for economic credibility remained low by 2015 and still does despite the failure of the Tory policy. Labour needs to be much more comfortable and confident in stressing an anti-austerity agenda and that does seem to be one area where the current leadership has developed a clear policy as the Shadow Chancellor, John McDonnell, has brought in a team of leading economists. However, although this is necessary it may not be sufficient unless the economy moves into recession as a response to international pressures and popular opinion moves more decisively against austerity.

Remaking the case for welfare – public opinion clearly moved decisively to a more critical view of welfare and welfare claimants under the

Thatcher and Major governments and despite the ever tougher rhetoric of both Conservative and Labour politicians has continued to do so. Indeed, it may be that there is a vicious circle here as tougher rhetoric from senior politicians in response to public opinion caused more public concern. Fiscal retrenchment since 2010 has been tied to the need to reduce the welfare burden. Conservative rhetoric about 'strivers not shirkers' sought to divide public opinion and win over populist support for austerity. The Labour Party can engage in this approach – and arguably should be more concerned with genuine cases of fraud than some on the liberal left would feel comfortable with – but it will always be outdone by the Conservatives if it plans to compete with them on this agenda. Instead, the Labour Party needs to set out a positive case for welfare based on the social and economic benefits of greater equality, the promotion of welfare rights, and the insurance principle whereby everyone contributes when they can and receive support when they need it. Some of the ways of doing this are explored by Robert M. Page, Pete Redford, Simon Griffiths and Judi Atkins. Welfare is not something that only applies to some and not others. The term 'welfare' itself has become derogatory and the idea I have outlined here would be better expressed through the more old-fashioned terminology of 'social security'. Given the pace of economic and technological change and the increased risk and uncertainty that the market and globalisation create, the positive case is that the welfare state provides the stability and security that people need at certain points in their lives. A small-c conservative defence of the welfare state – protecting people in the face of rapid and unsettling change – may be more fruitful than the more explicitly liberal defence of the welfare state which was the essence of the 'market liberal' view of the late 1980s and 1990s.

Identity – finally Labour needs to address the difficult area of identity politics. This has always been a difficult area for the left. Ever since Karl Marx wrote that nations were constructed identities masking the realities of class conflict and calling on 'workers of the world to unite' the left has viewed an attachment to the nation-state as something negative. Some have preferred to talk of class identity, others of a more liberal disposition have talked about citizenship. Meanwhile, the right were more comfortable talking about the nation. Some on the left regarded nationhood as an essentially backward emotional attachment. Even today there are some senior figures in the Labour Party who are critical of expressions of national identity, especially Englishness. Gordon Brown referred to Mrs Duffy as a 'bigoted woman' for expressing her concerns over immigration, while Emily Thornberry MP tweeted about the crude display of the flag of St George. Labour MPs seem happier talking about national identity when it is Welsh, Scottish or even Irish but not so English, which seems to be associated with both small 'c' and large 'C' Conservatism and memories of a lost Empire. One recent attempt to address this issue is that by so-called Blue Labour, but this was met with considerable scepticism in the Labour Party because of its essentially conservative tone and content. There are better guides for modern-day Labour to follow. It need only examine the postwar Labour Party ideology which was committed to both elements of the concept of the nation-state. The state had a positive role to play in both the management of the economy and the provision of social security, and the nation in terms of its fondness for British (as well as English, Scottish and Welsh) traditions and a commitment to strong defence and foreign policies. These themes are addressed well in this book by Jasper Miles and Matt Beech in particular, while Emily Robinson has looked at ways of reinvigorating the polity through constitutional reform and democratisation. What is certain given the decision to leave the EU is that identity politics becomes more important than ever for the Labour Party.

Therefore while some have become pessimistic following the 2015 general election defeat and the problems of social democracy elsewhere there are grounds for optimism. There is a route back for social democracy, or democratic socialism, if those who hold to that ideology can come up with convincing policies on the three areas outlined above – economic credibility, social protection and a greater acceptance of people's concerns about national identity of which this book has made a start. In order to do so Labour needs to be both confident in its own ideology and competent in terms of its policy package.

Index